MINORITY WOMEN AND AUSTERITY

Survival and resistance in France and Britain

Leah Bassel and Akwugo Emejulu

P

First published in Great Britain in 2018 by

Policy Press
University of Bristol
1-9 Old Park Hill
Bristol
BS2 8BB
UK
t: +44 (0)117 954 5940
pp-info@bristol.ac.uk
www.policypress.co.uk

North America office:
Policy Press
c/o The University of Chicago Press
1427 East 60th Street
Chicago, IL 60637, USA
t: +1 773 702 7700
f: +1 773-702-9756
sales@press.uchicago.edu
www.press.uchicago.edu

© Policy Press 2018

British Library Cataloguing in Publication Data
A catalogue record for this book is available from the British Library

Library of Congress Cataloging-in-Publication Data
A catalog record for this book has been requested

ISBN 978-1-4473-2714-1 paperback
ISBN 978-1-4473-2713-4 hardcover
ISBN 978-1-4473-2717-2 ePub
ISBN 978-1-4473-2718-9 Mobi
ISBN 978-1-4473-2716-5 ePdf

Cover design by Hayes Design
Front cover image: kindly supplied by Favianna Rodriguez
Printed and bound in Great Britain by CPI Group (UK) Ltd, Croydon, CR0 4YY
Policy Press uses environmentally responsible print partners

We dedicate this book to our grandmothers – Ollie Lee Mason and Adèle Fetterly – who, through their lives, taught us what survival and resistance means.

Contents

Glossary of French terms

adultes-relais	male or female intercultural mediators
banlieues	suburbs
bénéficiaires de l'Allocation de rentrée scolaire	Beneficiaries of Return to School Assistance
bénéficiaires de minima sociaux et d'aide au logement et prime	Beneficiaries of Minimum Social Assistance and Housing Assistance
cités	troubled housing estates
Code de l'Indigénat	The 'Code of the Indiginate'
communautarisme	the fear in France of breakdown into 'communities', leading to segregation and ghettoes
commune	the third tier of local government and administration in France, within *départements* and, in turn, the regions
Conseil national des villes	National Council of Cities
Délégation interministérielle à la ville	Inter-ministry Delegation responsible for cities
'*droit commun*'	common law/shared rights
enquêtes Emploi	employment surveys
Etat providence	welfare state
étrangers	foreigners
familles populaires	working-class families
femmes relais	literally 'relay women', or interpreters, intercultural mediators and intermediaries
Fichier Historique Statistique des Demandeurs d'Emploi	Statistical Record of Job Seekers
français de souche	white, native-born French
français issus de l'immigration	second-generation immigrant French

Front National	National Front
Haut conseil à l'intégration	High Council for Integration
Ined	National Institute for Demographic Studies
Insee	National Institute of Statistics and Economic Studies
laïc	secular, in the French sense
laïcité	French secularism
loi du travail	labour law
mal logés	the poorly housed
Marche de la dignité	The March for Dignity
Marche pour l'égalité et contre le racisme	The March for Equality and against Racism
métisse	mixed heritage
milieu associatif	the field of civil society organisations
milieu populaire	working-class area
militant/militantes	activists
minorités racialisés	racialised minorities
mouvement avorté	'aborted movement'
mouvement beur	'beur' (backslang for 'arabe') movement, anti-racist movement of the 1980s
Mouvement des Indigenes de la République	Movement of the Indigenous of the Republic
Ni Putes Ni Soumises	Neither Whores Nor Submissive
nivellement vers le bas	race to the bottom
non-remplacement	non-replacement
nouvelle pauvreté	'new poverty'
Nuit Debout	French social movement that began in 2016 against labour reforms
Observatoire national des zones urbaines sensibles	National observatory of 'sensitive' urban zones
parole	voice
Parti Socialiste	Socialist Party

politique de la ville	urban policy
quartiers	neighbourhoods
quartiers populaires	working-class neighbourhoods
quartiers sensibles	'sensitive' neighbourhoods or areas of the city
racaille	scum
racisme d'état	state racism
secteur caritatif	charitable/humanitarian sector
solidarité	solidarity
Union pour un Mouvement Populaire (UMP)	Union for a Popular Movement
verlan	backslang
zones urbaines sensibles (ZUS)	'sensitive' urban zones

About the authors

Leah Bassel is Associate Professor in Sociology at the University of Leicester. Her research interests include the political sociology of gender, migration, race and citizenship and she is author of *Refugee women: Beyond gender versus culture* (Routledge, 2012) and *The politics of listening: Possibilities and challenges for democratic life* (Palgrave, 2017). She conducted an Economic and Social Research Council-funded project 'The UK Citizenship Process: Exploring Immigrants' Experiences' and is Assistant Editor of the journal *Citizenship Studies*. Before her academic work, Leah was an emergency outreach worker with asylum seekers in Paris and created a circus camp project for young migrants.

Akwugo Emejulu is Professor of Sociology at the University of Warwick. Her research interests include the political sociology of race, gender and the grassroots activism of women of colour in Europe and America. Her first book, *Community development as micropolitics: Comparing theories, policies and politics in America and Britain* was published by Policy Press in 2015. Her work has appeared in *Politics & Gender, Race & Class* and the *Journal of Ethnic and Racial Studies*. Before entering academia, Akwugo worked as a community organiser, a participatory action researcher and as a trade-union organiser in America and Britain.

Acknowledgements

We would first like to thank all the women in France, England and Scotland who participated in this project. You took valuable time away from your busy lives to share your experiences with us. Your honesty, courage and commitment are an example to us and we hope to have done justice to you. While we are not mentioning you here by name to preserve anonymity, please know that you are far from nameless in our minds.

Second, we want to acknowledge the good fortune we have had in finding each other to work with in genuine collaboration. The sum was always greater than its parts and this book is the result of our endeavour to collectively think through the significance of these tough times. Note, we are equal contributors to this work.

Third, we gratefully acknowledge funding from the British Academy (Reference: SG112539) as well as the College of Social Sciences Research Development Fund, University of Leicester and the Centre for Education and Racial Equality in Scotland, University of Edinburgh.

Fourth, we come to the broad range of research assistants, colleagues and supporters who have our huge thanks:

Our research assistants – Ana Carillo-Lopez, Callum McGregor, Zakaria Sajir, Mirjam Twigt – who creatively as well as diligently helped us bring this work together, and Aleksander Nitka, who created a fabulous website for our project.

Our colleagues inside and outside of the academy who continuously supported and challenged us: Rowena Arshad, Philip Ayoub, Christine Bell, Mary Bernstein, Jenny Bourne, Julia Buxton, Sébastien Chauvin, Stuart Connor, Pauline Cullen, Jonathan Dean, Umut Erel, Liz Fekete, Robert Fisher, Don Flynn, Virginie Guiraudon, Toni Haastrup, Johanna Kantola, Indira Kartallozi, Kamran Khan, Maja Korac, Sabine Lang, Emanuela Lombardo, Madeleine Kennedy Macfoy, Nancy Naples, Gina Netto, Angela O'Hagan, Kirit Patel, David Paternotte, Kindy Sandhu, Sarah Shin, John Solomos, Hilary Sommerlad, Filip Sosenko, Gill Valentine, Mieke Verloo, Khursheed Wadia, Hazel Waters, Aaron Winter, Carol Young.

Finally, our friends and family, who stood by us throughout: Stella, Zoe, Yann, Kiki, Bill, George and auntie Emma; Duane, Emeka, Ngozi and Chika.

Foreword

Western democracies have long expressed a fascination with and disdain for the designated minority women in their midst. The category 'minority women' renders an array of non-white women simultaneously hypervisible in media yet silenced within important public-policy debates that shape their lives. For celebrities, hyper-visibility is a much-sought after commodity that catalyses fame and fortune, yet for Black, immigrant, Muslim, Latina, other women of colour and minority women, hyper-visibility fosters hyper-surveillance and discrimination. Across national contexts, which are shaped by intersecting power relations of racism, sexism, class exploitation and homophobia, minority women are seen but not heard. Instead a range of social actors speak both about and for minority women. This practice is not questioned. In fact such actors are seen as being better qualified to speak for minority women than the women themselves.

For those of us who are categorised as minority women, the public scrutiny that accompanies our hyper-visibility is rarely good news. We often become scapegoats for our respective societies' social problems as well as touchstones for fears and insecurities concerning national identity. As mothers, students, daughters and workers, minority women constitute the designated face of what's wrong with our respective societies. For example, women of colour in the US have been accused of an array of behaviours that ostensibly threaten the American way of life. Historically enduring, controlling images stigmatise Black women as being hyper-sexual, less intelligent, and morally lax, values that they purportedly pass on to their children. Latinas, especially undocumented immigrants, are rapidly joining Black women as a new threat. Latinas are accused of having too many babies, swelling the numbers of undeserving people who consume more than their fair share of American educational, health and family services. Muslim women who wear the hijab find themselves facing the threat of being physically attacked by perfect strangers. Unaware of or ignoring the heterogeneity among Muslim women, many Americans believe that Islam itself threatens national security. Collectively, these narratives effectively position women of colour as either incapable of assimilation (Black women), or as unwilling to assimilate (Latinas who do not speak English), or as harbingers of religious ideology that prevents them from assimilating. Such narratives may change in tandem with shifts in social and economic conditions, yet their role in upholding the economic, political and social subordination of women of colour remains constant. Minority women do not have problems – they cause problems and they are the problem.

What should minority women do in these national contexts, which put us on display, demonise us for some societal crisis, and then dismiss our ideas and actions in response to our discriminatory treatment? How do we claim and express political agency in fighting such uphill battles?

Minority women and austerity: Survival and resistance in France and Britain brings a breath of fresh air in grappling with these questions. Through careful and caring analysis of how minority women activists see and do politics, this volume sheds new light on the survival and resistance politics of minority women as subordinated social actors. As a scholar-activist who has both lived and worked in similar communities as the women interviewed for this book, and written about Black women and political activism, I recognised the women in *Minority women and austerity*. It was refreshing to see how Bassel and Emejulu examine not only the complexity of minority women activists' analyses of their work, but also how their political actions reflect sophisticated analyses of power. These women understand how power operates across race, gender, ethnicity, religion and class as intersecting systems of power, as well as how power organises the social institutions, disciplinary practices, cultural practices and interpersonal relations of their everyday lives.

I enjoyed reading *Minority women and austerity* because it provides much-needed evidence for how minority women both survive and resist their subordination. This excellent book has many themes that speak to issues in my own work, yet three stand out for me. First, I appreciated Bassel and Emejulu's decision to draw upon Black feminist analyses as foundational for how they framed their study. Traditional metrics of political participation simply do not work in explaining the political perspectives and actions of minority women. Black feminism has launched a sustained critique of the frameworks used to study Black women, as well as the epistemological underpinnings of those frameworks. In this context, the treatment of African American women as agents of knowledge instead of objects of knowledge signalled an important shift in US Black women's intellectual history. Via this approach, *Minority women and austerity* demonstrates a clear yet contentious break with dominant epistemological frameworks that over-emphasise minority women's status as devalued victims.

By drawing upon Black feminist frameworks and epistemologies, this book takes its rightful place within ongoing intellectual traditions by minority women who resist their political subordination. African American women, for example, created and sustained Black feminism as an intergenerational, culturally specific, intellectual and activist response to the forms that racism, sexism, and class and sexual exploitation took in the US. Yet despite the significance of this tradition, Black women's political analyses and actions within a US context are neither universal nor unique. Across diverse social contexts that ignore minority women's intellectual and political agency in confronting the social issues in our lives, minority women aim to carve out spaces of freedom, autonomy and political agency. *Minority women and austerity* contributes to this larger conversation about the contours of minority women's strategies for survival and resistance. But this conversation would have been less likely to occur were it not for the authors' decision to trust minority women as agents of knowledge in their own lives.

Second, I appreciated Bassel and Emejulu's decision to accept minority women activists as experts on their own lives. By studying activists, whether educated or not, across diverse political settings, the authors demonstrate how minority women working on behalf of their families, communities and their own wellbeing are the experts on their own experiences. Via this approach, the authors break with conventional scholarly wisdom concerning who counts as an expert and what kind of expertise is valued within academic and policy settings. The women who are interviewed in this book do not need others to explain their situations to them. Rather, the women activists seek a forum where they can step back and reflect on the ideas and actions that emerge within their everyday lives. We get a different view of how political theory emerges from within the crucible of political actions, rather than political theory that reflects the norms of disengaged scholarly experts.

Bassel and Emejulu's decision to redefine minority women's knowledge as expert knowledge enables them to avoid the trap of replicating hierarchies within their study of minority women's resistance traditions. Within gender, race and class hierarchies, men speak for and about women, whites routinely study minority groups, and intellectuals from elite groups are seen as more qualified to analyse the actions of ordinary, everyday folks. The social hierarchies that characterise gender, race and class as intersecting systems of power reproduce social scripts about who is an expert and who is not. Among women, educated elite women routinely speak for their more disadvantaged sisters, with race and class mapping onto patterns of privilege and penalty.

Less-educated minority women are expected to respect the expertise of their superiors. I like this book because it avoids this trap. Given the subject matter of this project – investigating political resistance by subordinated social actors – making sure that a broad constellation of minority women, not just educated or famous minority women, are the experts becomes especially important.

Finally, I really appreciated how *Minority women and austerity* focused on how three distinctive national settings provided different political contexts for minority women's political behaviour. The national contexts that shape the political actions of minority women constitute an important dimension of survival and resistance, yet such contexts are often taken for granted. France, England and Scotland have different histories concerning how women experience discrimination as minority women, and even who counts as a minority woman. As a result, women across these national contexts share similar overall challenges that take distinctive forms within each nation state. There is no one-size-fits-all version of minority women's politics. Instead, political processes of survival and resistance are fundamentally contextual.

Refusing to collapse minority women into an undifferentiated mass in which one group's experiences can easily substitute for those of another brings greater depth to the book's analysis of minority women's politics of survival and resistance. Standard social-science research routinely compares white and minority women, often with the implicit assumption that white women constitute the norm. In fact, the very category of 'minority women' raises the question, who are the majority women? In contrast, this book eschews this dominant race-relations frame in favour of an alternative framework that investigates the differences among minority women. When it comes to questions of survival and resistance, this shift allows entirely new topics of investigation to come into view. Moreover, this book makes an important contribution to ongoing efforts to build a rich repository of similar projects by minority women that potentially facilitate a more robust politics of survival and resistance. With access to studies like this one, minority women across varying national contexts might be better positioned to develop increasingly complex and effective political responses to sexism, racism, class exploitation and homophobia.

Failing to see minority women as expert political analysts and actors perpetuates their subordination. But if we are brave enough to ask new questions, to recognise the difference between being silenced by dominant institutions and minority women's strategic decisions to remain silent and/or speak out when necessary, we begin to understand how the politics of subordinated groups within democratic societies actually work. In this endeavour, *Minority women and austerity* offers some important guidance.

Patricia Hill Collins
University of Maryland, College Park
May 2017

ONE

Taking minority women's activism seriously

Introduction

The 2008 economic crisis and subsequent austerity measures represent a contradictory moment for minority women in France and Britain. On the one hand, the 'crisis' is not necessarily a new experience for these women. In pre-crisis France and Britain, minority women were already in precarious social and economic circumstances (Emejulu 2008; Bassel 2012). Regardless of their educational outcomes, minority women were – and continue to be – more likely to be unemployed, underemployed or over-concentrated in low-skilled, low-paid, insecure employment (Emejulu 2008; Seguino 2010; Women's Budget Group 2010). A striking feature of the crisis is that more privileged groups are now starting to experience the routine crises and precarity that minority women have long had to negotiate. On the other hand, however, crisis and austerity do represent an important change in the material circumstances of minority women. Due to the asymmetrical impacts of austerity, minority women are disproportionately disadvantaged by cuts to public spending thus sharpening and deepening their existing inequalities (Theodoropoulou and Watt 2011; APPG 2012; Emejulu and Bassel 2013).

Despite minority women's routinised experiences of inequality, they are not passive objects at the mercy of economic restructurings and particular policy priorities. Minority women, often operating in hostile contexts among ostensible allies, are organising and mobilising in innovative ways to advance their intersectional social justice claims (Bassel and Emejulu 2014; Emejulu and Bassel 2013; Emejulu and Bassel 2015). Building on our cross-national research project *Minority Women's Activism in Tough Times*, this book examines minority women's experiences of, and activism within, the austerity regimes of France and Britain. Through in-depth case studies of the particular dynamics of austerity and activism in Scotland, England and France, we explore how activists operate in this moment of political and economic uncertainty and practice a 'politics of survival' (Hill Collins 2000).

In this introductory chapter, we discuss the three national contexts in which our research project was based, highlighting the particular citizenship regimes of each country and the implications for our minority women activists (see Table 1.1 at the end of this chapter for a summary of case characteristics). We then move on to provide further details about the research, detailing our methods, sampling, participant characteristics and coding and analysis frame. We define the key terms that we will be using throughout this book. Finally, we conclude with an overview of how the 2008 economic crisis and subsequent austerity measures impacted on minority and migrant women in France and Britain.

The three cases: France, England and Scotland

Our book aims to situate minority women's experiences of and activism against austerity in three different national contexts: France, England and Scotland. The book builds on our previous work exploring minority women's claims-making for equality in France and Britain (Bassel and Emejulu 2010). In the literature on citizenship regimes in France and Britain, these two countries are often constructed as opposites.

In France, the republican 'model' of citizenship requires that private identity, expressly linked to race, ethnicity and religion, should not play a political role in the public sphere. *Laïcité*, which roughly translates as 'secularism', acts as an organising principle of the French Republic, codifying the norms in public space. The underlying ideology of the French citizenship 'model' is difference blindness: each citizen has the same rights and responsibilities in public and is an equal, abstract entity before the law. It is extremely difficult, but not impossible, for minority groups to name 'race' in their activism, because institutional actors construct these claims and identities as illegitimate. These claims seek to break down the boundaries between private and public space that are premised on a racial order in which racialised Others are not political subjects, and minority women are audible only as victims but never equal citizens (Bassel 2012). In this book, we chart how minority women activists negotiate this challenging context: sometimes negotiation results in endorsing Republican logic at the cost of being instrumentalised, while other activists challenge the 'political racelessness' that we explore in Chapter Two, and make intersectional social justice claims based on their own terms which name race, gender, ethnicity, religion and legal status.

In contrast, the British 'model' is explicitly multicultural – although the multiculturalist principle appears to be in retreat in England. The assumption of the British idea of citizenship is that liberal pluralism leads to a stronger and more legitimate democracy. Multiculturalism protects the individual rights and freedoms of minority groups and enables these groups to participate effectively in civil society. Rather than promoting assimilation into the normative values of a state, as in the French model, the focus in Britain is on extending the benefits of citizenship to different kinds of individuals, thus further strengthening democracy. This idea of liberal pluralism is being increasingly contested, however, and we are witnessing important divergences between England and Scotland in relation to multicultural citizenship and a broader questioning of 'models' that we return to in Chapter Six.

England, like other European countries, is experiencing a backlash against multiculturalism that spans both the political Left and the Right (Modood 2013; Kymlicka 2010; Colombo 2015). This backlash is fuelled by an existential crisis of national identity, in which multiculturalism is perceived by both the public and politicians as eroding 'shared British values' and threatening 'traditional ways of life' (Joppke 2004). On the Right, this backlash has, in part, fostered the rise of the Eurosceptic and anti-immigrant United Kingdom Independence Party, whose surprise success in the Brexit campaign shook the political scene as this manuscript was finalised.

On the Left, key architects and proponents of multicultural citizenship, such as the former head of the Equality and Human Rights Commission, Trevor Phillips, and three former Labour Home Secretaries, David Blunkett, Jack Straw and John Reid, have all recanted their former positions and claim that multiculturalism unintentionally reinforces minority groups' social isolation and exclusion (Phillips 2005). The changing fortunes of multicultural citizenship in England has created a difficult environment for the minority women activists in our study. While they are more able to advance social justice claims based on their race, ethnicity, religion and legal status, unlike our French activists, questions remain as to how and whether these claims are heard by social movement allies and by institutional actors alike.

Scotland provides an interesting counterpoint to both England and France in terms of its citizenship regime. Like England, it shares the principle of liberal pluralism and actively promotes an idea of Scottish multicultural citizenship. Like the rest of Europe, Scotland is also experiencing an upturn in nationalist sentiment. In stark contrast to other European countries, however, Scotland combines its nationalism with multiculturalism to advance a civic multicultural nationalism and national identity. As Emejulu argues:

> Scottish nationalism as a political project is not typically practised on nativist terms. Indeed, the dominant form of Scottish nationalism as evidenced in the Scottish National Party (SNP) has deliberately pursued an inclusive form of national identity that is not solely tied to blood and birth but a commitment to Scottish self-determination and independence. (Emejulu 2013: 46)

The Scottish independence referendum consolidated this distinctive political milieu in that the governing Scottish National Party (SNP), as well as other pro-independence movements and parties such as the Commonweal, the Radical Independence Campaign, the Scottish Greens and the Scottish Socialist Party, advanced clear anti-racist and pro-migrant positions during the campaign. However, it is important not to overstate Scottish politics in relation to citizenship and multiculturalism. As McCrone and Bechhofer (2008: 172) note, because Scotland has not experienced a large wave of migration and settlement of people of colour, racist and xenophobic debates about identity and citizenship are not 'politically active categories' for popular debate at this moment in time. The Scottish population remains overwhelmingly white – this group constitutes 98% of the population (Scotland's Census 2013). Because elite discourse is dominated by an inclusive national identity, a political entrepreneur has, as yet, been unsuccessful in translating a more exclusive and xenophobic form of nationalism into electoral success. Thus, Scottish politics have not yet been 'tested' in a context of a genuinely multiracial and multi-ethnic society. As we will demonstrate in the following chapters, the minority women activists in our study do not seem to have substantially benefited from this seemingly open and welcoming political environment. Indeed, their experiences, despite the rhetoric of inclusion and multiculturalism in Scotland, echo in significant ways the problems of silence and erasure that their counterparts in England and France experience.

In this book, we try to understand minority women's activism as determined by, but also challenging, the particular discursive and material opportunity structures in each country. We take seriously both the constraints and the opportunities that the specific political milieux generate for our activists, but we also seek to understand their experiences and activism in the context of debates about race, citizenship and austerity in Europe. In the subsequent chapters, we will make clear those experiences that are case-specific and those that appear to be shared across France, England and Scotland. We aim to understand the discrete but complementary ways in which processes of racialised and gendered exclusion are reproduced in civil society and in policy making in Europe. Our case studies illuminate the diverse ways in which minority women activists assert their agency as political subjects and problematise their exclusion from the European polity.

Methods

From September 2011 to May 2014, we conducted 55 semi-structured, one-to-one interviews with:

- minority and migrant activist women;
- directors, policy officers and development workers in anti-poverty, housing and migrant rights third sector organisations;
- civil servants and local government officials with a brief for equalities and/or the third sector in Glasgow, Edinburgh, Manchester, Coventry, London, Paris and Lyon.

We also conducted one focus group with activist minority women in Glasgow. We included a combination of capital cities (London, Paris and Edinburgh) and important regional cities (Manchester, Lyon, Coventry) in order to avoid the bias toward capital cities, which obscures regional dynamics and the problems and possibilities activists face when working in less dense associational networks. We have indicated these effects within cases as well as across them. Although, note, Glasgow defies this classification, because it is the largest city in Scotland and has the largest minority ethnic population in the country.

In addition, in a separate but related project about the impact of austerity on different minority ethnic groups in Glasgow, we also conducted three focus groups of approximately seven to ten participants each with minority and migrant women about their experiences of austerity (For a detailed analysis of these specific findings see: Sosenko et al 2013).[1] We also organised two knowledge exchange events – 'Whose Crisis Counts?' in Edinburgh in June 2013 and '21st Century London Outcasts' in London in February 2014 – over the course of the project. These brought together 55 practitioners, activists, civil servants and academics, and fed directly into our data collection and ongoing analysis. We draw from our notes and observations of these events as well, in discussing minority women's experiences throughout the book. The Appendix provides further details of our fieldwork and sampling strategy, key characteristics of participants cited and location, and our process of analysis and coding frame.

All the interviews and the focus group focused on four key themes:

- how participants conceptualised the economic crisis and austerity;
- what impact they thought the crisis was having on them and/or their organisation;
- what impact the crisis was having on minority women's activism; and
- what impact crisis and austerity was having on the ability to influence policy makers.

All participants' names have been changed and any details that would allow their organisations to be recognised have also been omitted.

We brought all these data together for the purpose of our analysis. Following transcription, we developed a coding frame that was adapted across all three cases to account for important contextual variation. This involved identifying emergent categories and themes as well as the themes that had been derived deductively, justifying case studies across the diverse contexts in Britain and France.

Inevitably, our data are not equally balanced across our three cases. Given that we used snowball sampling techniques to recruit participants into our study, there are gaps in our sample, in which we have over-sampled in some places and under-sampled in others. In discussing our findings, we will make clear where our data are incomplete, where readers should treat some findings with caution and what further research is required. As this is a relatively small-scale qualitative study, we do not claim to represent the entire national context in France, England or Scotland, but instead we point to differences in our data and consider what these differences may imply more generally in relation to minority women's anti-austerity activism.

Defining and operationalising key terms

By 'minority women', we refer to women who experience the effects of processes of racialisation, class and gender domination as well as other sources of inequality, particularly hierarchies of legal status. It is a term we have chosen to use in that we think it travels best across our three cases and also across the different types of women of colour we have included in our study. For instance, 'Black and minority ethnic' is a term that predominates in Britain but is not used in France. 'Of immigrant origin' is widely used in France but not in Britain, and we do not wish to reproduce problematic language when discussing race and ethnicity in a European context. As North Americans working in Britain, we prefer the term 'women of colour', but acknowledge that this label is seen by some as a problematic importation of North American race politics. We do not seek to impose this identity on the participants in our study, so we have opted to use the labels they use to describe themselves. Thus, 'minority women' seems to be the best way of referring to a heterogeneous group of women who have differing migration histories and citizenship statuses. How to name the women in our study matters; what we are interested in exploring in this book are the processes that produce 'minority' status rather than an essentialised understanding of identity.

We recruited 'minority women activists' into our study who identified and described themselves in the following ways. In the English and Scottish contexts, we included women who self-identify as 'Black', a label they use politically. In the French, Scottish and English contexts, we included women who self-identify as 'refugee' or 'migrant', or who refer to organisations with names including these labels – women who, in the course of interviews, refer to their own identity or background by saying for example: 'I am of immigrant origin' (*d'origine immigrée* in France); 'my family is from …'.

Our participants also include self-identified advocates of specific groups of women, for example: refugees, asylum seekers and migrants. These advocates were sometimes part of the white mainstream – our French sample in particular has a high representation of 'French' advocates – and sometimes also self-identified minority women, or women who situated themselves as 'advocates', though also belonging to a minority group they were discussing. Some participants identified as minority women who, while minoritised along some axes, were advantaged along others, in terms of a higher socioeconomic status through professional employment and higher education qualifications. In some cases, more advantaged minority women specifically identified their class position as a resource from which they could draw in order to effectively advocate on behalf of other minority women (for example from their own ethnic group).

We focus on activism in and around third sector organisations. The difficulty of defining the term 'third sector' is well documented in the literature (see, for example, Vakil 1997; Martens 2002). The plethora of terms used to describe the sector reflect this difficulty: 'third sector', 'charities', 'voluntary sector', 'civil society organisations', 'community-based organisations', 'associations', 'non-governmental organisations'. We refer here to 'formal (professionalised) independent societal organisations whose primary aim is to promote common goals at the national or the international level' (Martens 2002: 280) as well as organisations oriented to the local and regional level. We include a normative element in both our definition and analysis: it is our position that these organisations have the potential to represent principles of mutuality, solidarity and independence from the state and the market (although this is not a necessary element of defining these organisations more broadly). As Aziz Choudry and Eric Shragge (2011: 506) note, 'NGOs operate in so many contexts and roles that it is difficult to generalize about them'. Our sample selection is, therefore, informed by this definition but, in turn, enables us to refine a more context-specific understanding of the organisations we study.

In our selection of 'third sector organisations' to include in our study, we wanted to ensure that we had a sample that reflected the diversity and the spectrum of activity that typically characterises the third sector in the three countries. Thus, we included organisations that are:

- traditional social welfare service providers;
- hybrid organisations combining advocacy and campaigning with service provision;
- organisations offering so-called 'militant provision' – crisis relief and political organising for destitute and/or undocumented migrants;
- campaigning and policy advocacy organisations that are not involved in service provision and are closer to social movements in that they situate their activity at the edge of social service provision and also as part of 'a network of informal interactions'. (Diani 1992: 8)

We intentionally have not made gender equality/feminist organisations the focus of our sample, though some are included, because the bulk of research about women's grassroots activism focuses on explicitly feminist organising (Sudbury 1998; Dominelli 2006; Annesley 2012), and we feel that the responsibility for recognising and advancing minority women's social justice claims does not only rest on feminist shoulders. Our focus is on the extent to which social action and activism within so-called 'mainstream' organisations involves and intersects with minority women's concerns and activism.

We define 'activism' broadly in order to capture the diverse ways in which minority women assert themselves as political agents. Minority women have distinctive patterns to their political behaviour that are often ignored, misrecognised or devalued in the wider political science literature and in the formal practice of politics (Sudbury 1998; Hill Collins 2000; Emejulu and Bassel 2015). 'Political behaviour' is typically defined as political participation in formal institutional structures and organised political activities. Thus voting, being a political party or trade union activist, taking part in demonstrations and standing for election are usually what counts as legitimate political action. Because minority women are underrepresented in these traditional political spaces, it appears as if minority women are absent from politics, or worse, operate largely as apolitical agents. It is only when we redefine 'what counts' as politics and political behaviour that the diverse ways in which minority women undertake political action becomes visible. As Patricia Hill Collins (2000: 201) argues: 'survival is a form of resistance and … struggles to provide for the survival of … children represent the foundations of Black women's activism'. Certainly, Hill Collins is analysing the particular history of African American women's resistances, but her wider point about the need to recognise and value the political actions of Black women in both public *and private* spaces is central to our understandings of minority women's political behaviour in Europe. Indeed, we chose to call the activism that we charted in our study 'the politics of survival' in order to capture, recognise and help to legitimise the spectrum of resistances that minority women are undertaking and extend the moniker of 'activist' to as many women as possible.

In this book, we chart minority women's activism in formalised third sector organisations but also in informal self-help groups, grassroots community organisations, trade unions and social movements. While our work focuses on action in and around the third sector, some participants were involved in more militant and radical organising and actions (and some even involved in both), and we attempt to reflect this range of experience.

Intersectionality and activists' social justice claims

Intersectionality is at the heart of this project. We define intersectionality as 'the study of the simultaneous and interacting effects of gender, race, class, sexual orientation, and national origin as categories of difference' (Bassel and Emejulu 2010: 518). We have argued elsewhere that an 'intersectional' move is urgently needed to challenge state representations of the crisis and the silencing of alternative analyses that demonstrate its differential and asymmetrical impacts (Bassel and Emejulu 2014; Emejulu and Bassel 2015). The idea of intersectionality forces us to confront and think about women and men in complex and heterogeneous ways. Exploring how gender, ethnicity, race, class, disability, age, religion and sexuality interact in different ways, depending on different national contexts, is crucial in seeking to construct a state that supports and recognises multiple social justice claims (see also Strolovitch 2007).

In this book, we argue that to understand minority women's experiences of the crisis and their resistances to it requires the simultaneous consideration of processes of racialisation and hierarchies of legal status, ability and other processes of stratification which exist *alongside* and are *inflected by* gender inequalities and are, in turn, exacerbated by austerity measures. We wish not only to identify the differential effects of austerity measures on various social groups, but also to support new examinations of – and oppositions to – neoliberal hegemony, and how minority women are – and can be – the authors and leaders of such oppositions.

Specifically, we explore how race, class, gender and legal status interact and shape both minority women's grassroots anti-austerity activism in each country and what kinds of claims and political actors are recognised and legitimated by both policy makers and civil society allies. Intersectional claims are not the only forms of opposition, and not all the activist women in our study were making (or particularly interested in) intersectional claims. Indeed, a number of activists were advancing single axis claims related to racial justice or migrants' rights, for example, or adopted 'difference blind' Republic stances in France. Furthermore, intersectional claims are advanced not only by minority women but also by their allies, in ways that are sometimes problematic. Our interest is in who is audible and legitimate and how these hierarchies of knowledge and political credibility are reproduced or overthrown. Centring minority women's articulations of both crisis and resistance is a way to subvert the dominant narrative of both 'crisis' and 'activism'.

We will now turn to examine the 2008 economic crisis, the policy response of austerity and the impact on minority women in France, England and Scotland.

The 2008 economic crisis, austerity measures and minority women

The origins of the 2008 economic crisis can be traced back to the liberalisation of finance since the 1980s. The current crisis 'derives from the long-term consequences of a cluster of financial innovations that aimed to separate credit decisions from their subsequent risks by splitting them into various components' (Boyer 2012: 285). In other words, the creation of synthetic financial instruments – the now infamous credit default swaps and collateralised debt obligations – separated investors' decision-making from their associated risks. This fuelled 'a private credit-led speculative boom' (Boyer 2012: 285), which ultimately proved unsustainable once the key manifestation of supposedly risk-free speculation – America's subprime mortgage market – went into freefall.

What is important in our analysis of the effects of the economic crisis on minority women is the way in which the causes of the crisis and the range of possible policy responses to the crisis have been subsequently misrepresented by institutional actors and financial elites in both France and Britain. Here we draw the broader picture, and in Chapter Three we explore specific measures and policies in greater depth.

The policies of austerity – deficit reduction through tax increases and cuts to public spending – are typically framed as the painful consequence of out-of-control state spending rather than as the result of states rescuing irresponsible financial institutions. Consequently, austerity has been represented by institutional actors as the only viable economic policy in order to get states' 'fiscal houses in order'. As Clarke and Newman (2012: 300) argue, institutional actors and financial elites are undertaking 'intense ideological work' to reframe how the public thinks about the causes of the crisis and to win the public's 'disaffected consent' for deeply unpopular austerity policies. Part of this ideological work is the 'magical thinking' of instituting paradoxical austerity policies that have 'contractionary effects' on the economy (Clarke and Newman 2012: 302-3). By contractionary effects, they mean that by undertaking an unprecedented programme of cuts, this massive withdrawal of state spending will actually further shrink economic output rather than jumpstart economic growth and job creation. Indeed, the fact that during our fieldwork the International Monetary Fund, the Organisation for Economic Co-operation and Development and the European Council all called for a rethink of austerity policies – given the shrinking economies and weak recoveries both inside and outside the Eurozone – appears to support these claims (Wearden 2013). Britain's vote to leave the European Union in June 2016 has served to heighten uncertainties for both the Eurozone and the global economy.

Britain is undergoing the most extensive reduction and restructuring of its welfare state since the Second World War (Taylor-Gooby and Stoeker 2010; Yeates et al 2011; Taylor-Gooby 2011; Whiteley et al 2014). During the five-year Conservative–Liberal Democrat Coalition government from 2010 to 2015, £80 billion spending cuts were announced that included £18 billion reduction in welfare spending

(Brewer and Browne 2011: 4). The Conservative–Liberal Democrat Coalition government presided over a 27% cut to local government – the key mechanism for delivery of public services – and a 68% cut to the social housing budget (Taylor-Gooby 2011: 4). These spending cuts are 'larger than any retrenchment since the 1920s' (Taylor-Gooby 2011: 4). With the unexpected Conservative victory at the polls in May 2015, the then Prime Minister David Cameron and the then Chancellor of the Exchequer, George Osborne, announced a further £12 billon reduction in social welfare spending. Theresa May's Conservative government, newly in power following the Brexit referendum, has not advanced a clear economic policy at the time of going to press (September 2016) beyond a statement abandoning George Osborne's commitment to generate a budget surplus by the next general election scheduled for 2020.

The SNP government at Holyrood opposes the Westminster austerity programme and has an official policy of mitigating its impact in Scotland through a combination of its Social Wage and the full mitigation of the so-called 'bedroom tax' (Scottish Government 2015). Under the current devolution settlement, however, the Scottish government is obliged to implement these dramatic spending cuts.

While France has not implemented as stringent austerity measures in comparison to Britain, a key aim of the *Parti Socialiste* government is deficit reduction and cuts to public spending. François Hollande came to power during our fieldwork, generating both optimism and cynicism from our participants. His flagship redistributive measure of a 75% 'supertax' on households with incomes over €1 million, key to his campaign, was dropped, returning to a top marginal income tax rate of 45% in 2015. The Socialist government did not opt for sweeping cuts but, instead, made reductions via a freeze on all government spending, which effectively cut public spending. Hollande's approach has since shifted to the centre: while in early 2016 he proposed a €2 billion fund for 500,000 training schemes for the unemployed, he has also implemented policies such as tax breaks for companies to reduce unemployment. Most controversially, changes to labour law through the *loi travail* bring France 'closer' to Britain in weakening employment protections for workers and making trade union consultations expendable in negotiating working conditions. These drastic changes to working conditions were the initial impetus for the *Nuit Debout* movement. We review in greater detail in Chapter Three the different phases and measures adopted in the French austerity regime.

What do the austerity regimes in France and Britain mean for minority women? Despite initial reports of a 'he-cession', women, and minority women in particular, appear to be disproportionately impacted by the crisis and the cuts (Women's Budget Group 2010). Under austerity, minority women are disproportionately disadvantaged due to their already existing precarity, compounded by their particular relationships with the social welfare state. In Chapter Three we demonstrate minority women's institutionalised precarity pre- and post-crisis. Minority women are more likely to be employed in the public sector (as teachers, nurses and social workers, for example), more likely to be subcontracted to the state via private sector organisations (for example, as care workers, cleaners and caterers) and are also more likely to be connected to the local state (through accessing public services), because of gendered caring responsibilities (Taylor-Gooby 2011; APPG 2012; Duhamel and Joyeux 2013). Therefore, austerity measures clearly increase minority women's unemployment, while simultaneously reducing the scope and coverage of public services, as well as women's access to such services. Reports on the impact of measures such as the Universal Credit and the Bedroom Tax in England, piloted in April 2013 in London boroughs where some of our research was conducted, indicate a disproportionate impact on women, particularly survivors of domestic violence. These cuts and their impacts been powerfully challenged by Sisters Uncut, a British feminist collective, and we explore their actions further in Chapter Six.[2]

Given that both minority women's economic insecurity and activism are erased from popular and political understandings of the crisis and austerity, this book seeks to centre minority women's experiences and resistances in France, England and Scotland.

Outline of the book

We begin, in **Chapter Two,** by examining the construction of 'political racelessness' (Goldberg 2006: 336) in Europe, and how it is reproduced and legitimised in ways that violently erase and exclude minority women and their interests from the European polity. Minority women must negotiate a hostile political context, in which their intersectional social justice claims are often rendered invisible and inaudible. Political racelessness, we argue, is not only a project of the reactionary Right in Europe. The European socialist and social democratic Left also deploy political racelessness in order to further its twin – although contradictory – project of economic populism, by appealing to a raceless and genderless 'people' and by reasserting the importance of a unified (and presumably all white) 'working class'.

In **Chapters Three to Six** we discuss in detail the empirical contours of this misrecognition and invisibility – but also minority women's resistances.

In **Chapter Three** we examine in detail minority women's institutionalised precarity in pre- and post-crisis France, England and Scotland. Using the framework of intersectionality, we demonstrate how minority women, a heterogeneous group, experience systematic discrimination and multidimensional inequalities based on their race, class, gender and legal status. We also explore the particular ways in which minority women are rendered either invisible or hypervisible in key social policies meant to address their routinised inequalities. Even though minority women experience systemic social and economic inequalities, too often their experiences are erased or devalued. The 2008 crisis and subsequent austerity measures do not represent a fundamentally new experience of precarity for minority women; rather, this is a sharpening and deepening of their already existing inequalities. We argue that we must resist the temptation of using a policy frame of a 'new' crisis as an explanation of minority women's inequalities, as this actually has the effect of erasing their experiences and re-inscribing those of the economically privileged.

In **Chapter Four** we explore how the changing politics of the third sector under austerity problematises minority women's intersectional social justice claims in Scotland, England and France. In particular, we examine how the transformation of the third sector in each country into a 'governable terrain' (Carmel and Harlock 2008) for state social welfare service delivery entrenches an 'enterprise culture' that valorises neoliberal principles and behaviours, which in turn undermines and misrecognises minority women's claims-making. The idea of enterprise has become entrenched within these organisations, and problematically reshapes the ways in which organisations think about their mission, practices and programmes of work – especially in relation to minority women. The ability for minority women to articulate and take action on intersectional social justice claims within the sector is under threat, because these claims may well be silenced and/or misrecognised due to the prevailing neoliberal logic of the sector.

In **Chapter Five** we explore minority women's strategies for survival in informal spaces: self-help groups, DIY networks and grassroots community organisations, as well as our participants' personal narratives of, and reflections on, coping within neoliberal third sector organisations. We seek to redefine 'what counts' and who enjoys the identity of 'activist', by naming and analysing minority women's politics of survival. Recognising and valuing the political actions of minority women in both public and private spaces is central to our understandings of minority women's political behaviour in Europe. We centre the activism of minority women and note that it is often connected to third sector spaces and should not be dismissed as 'inauthentic' for this reason. Yet we also demonstrate that no space is immune from 'enterprise', and show the ways in which context matters in each case to limit as well as frame minority women's activism as a politics of survival.

In **Chapter Six** we take a step back to think across our three cases, and beyond them. We reflect on our cases in order to avoid the analytical straightjacket of national 'models' that can obscure similarities as much as they also elucidate differences between France, England and Scotland. We then move 'beyond' them, in the sense of thinking about the internationalist and autonomous dimensions of intersectional and minority women-led organising that we see in the creative, subversive and influential voices and actions of new actors and movements in both France and Britain.

We conclude with **Chapter Seven,** where we sound a further warning as the European racial contract becomes more overtly hateful and legitimate, with profound implications for minority women. The 'burkini ban' and the mass and disproportionate of Muslim citizens following terrorist attacks in France; the spike in racist attacks following the Brexit vote in England; and the complacency and smugness of Scottish nationalism that supplants discussions of intersectional social justice claims: all these issues play out against the backdrop of the European migration 'crisis'. Minority women are once again pathologically present but politically absent, but it is through a politics of survival that some minority women denounce this political racelessness and advance their interests on their own terms.

We now turn to explore the European racial contract and its (re) production of political racelessness.

Table 1.1: Case characteristics

	Austerity regime	Approach to diversity	Third sector characteristics
England	Top-down 'voluntary austerity' programme initiated by the 2010 Conservative–Liberal Democrat Coalition government (benefits cap, 'bedroom tax', changes to disability benefits).[3]	Multiculturalism in retreat; Single Equalities Body, Equalities Duty and Equality Impact Assessments as codified in the Equality Act 2010. London, where most of this research was conducted, is the most ethnically diverse area across England and Wales, according to the 2011 Census.[4]	Important part of the 'welfare mix', with service delivery organisations competing for contracts but also an array of oppositional/campaigning organisations. A vibrant, but increasingly precarious, Black and Minority Ethnic third sector.
France	Confused and continuously shifting approach to austerity. Moderate austerity measures initially proposed by the *Parti Socialiste* government followed by a shift to the Right.	Ostensible 'difference blindness', which is actively and controversially enforced through conventions such as *laïcité*. Paris, where most of this research was conducted, is the most ethnically diverse city, with high levels of racial segregation.	Have grown in importance since the 1980s as key partners in tackling *la nouvelle pauvreté* and the *mouvement beur*. No recognised Black and Minority Ethnic third sector, but a long history of migrant mobilisation within the *milieu associatif* and de facto ethno-specific organisations.[5]
Scotland	Anti-austerity SNP government seeks to mitigate Westminster-driven austerity policies, using its limited welfare powers under the current devolution agreement.	Explicit multiculturalism as part of Scottish nationalist project. A smaller minority ethnic population than England or France. Groups are concentrated in the largest cities, Edinburgh and Glasgow, where this research was conducted[6] (although 12% of Glasgow's population is from a minority ethnic background, as recorded in the 2011 Census).	The third sector is an important player in the delivery of public services but is also represented by an array of oppositional/campaigning organisations. A small, precarious but recognised Black and Minority Ethnic third sector.

Notes

[1] When quoting participants in the study, we refer to them as 'Coalition for Racial Equality and Rights (CRER) Participant X'. Further details of participants can be found in the fieldwork appendix (Appendix).

[2] See: *The Guardian* 19 June 2013 and Sisters Uncut: www.sistersuncut.org/

[3] Changes include: the introduction of 'Universal Credit', a cap on benefits that working-age people can receive, introduction of the 'bedroom tax' (a cut to the amount of benefit that people can get if they are deemed to have a spare bedroom in their council or housing association home); introduction of the Personal Independence Payment, which will replace the Disability Living Allowance. See: https://www.gov.uk/government/policies/simplifying-the-welfare-system-and-making-sure-work-pays and for impact assessment, the National Housing Federation: www.housing.org.uk/policy/welfare-reform/bedroom-tax#sthash.kumEFRu2.dpuf

[4] London was the most ethnically diverse area, with the highest proportion of minority ethnic groups and the lowest proportion of the White ethnic group at 59.8% in 2011 (Office for National Statistics 2012).

[5] France does not collect statistics on ethnicity, a source of longstanding debate (Sabbagh and Peer 2008; Simon 2008a 2008b).

[6] The size of the minority ethnic population in 2011 was just over 200,000 or 4% of the total population of Scotland (based on the 2011 ethnicity classification); this has doubled since 2001, when just over 100,000 or 2% of the total population of Scotland (based on the 2001 ethnicity classification) were from a minority ethnic group (Scotland's Census 2013).

TWO

Theorising and resisting 'political racelessness' in Europe

Introduction

In this chapter, we set the scene for our empirical examination of minority women's misrecognition and invisibility – but also minority women's resistances. We examine political racelessness in Europe, which is reproduced and legitimised in ways that violently erase and exclude minority women and their interests from the European polity. We take the concept of 'political racelessness' from David Theo Goldberg, who defines it as a key element of 'racial Europeanisation', in which 'race is to have no social place, no explicit markings. It is to be excised from any characterising of human conditions, relations [or] formations' (Goldberg 2006: 336). Europe seeks to abolish race epistemologically and empirically through a process of forgetting its colonial history and disavowing its ongoing postcolonial entanglements with those it classes as 'Others' within its borders.

Minority women must negotiate a hostile political context, in which their intersectional social justice claims are often rendered invisible and inaudible. For minority women activists in particular, they must confront their erasure from both the political Right and Left. Indeed, as we will go on to argue, political racelessness is not only a project of the reactionary Right in Europe. The European socialist and social democratic Left also actively deploys political racelessness to further its twin – although contradictory – project of economic populism, by appealing to a raceless and genderless 'people' and by reasserting the importance of a unified (and presumably all white) 'working class'.

We begin this chapter with a discussion of why political racelessness is a central feature of postcolonial amnesia in Europe. We move on to discuss how political racelessness is achieved and defended in Europe through the cultivation of 'white ignorance' (Mills 2007) and 'white innocence' (Wekker 2016). We then turn to examine how the white European Left – despite a long tradition of anti-racist and anti-fascist resistance – perpetuates political racelessness at the expense of minority groups and minority women in particular. We conclude with a discussion about how we might theorise minority women's activism in a context of white ignorance in Europe.

The racial logic of Europe

Making racial justice claims is extremely difficult to achieve and sustain in Europe, because of Europe's commitment to political racelessness. As we demonstrate throughout this book, political racelessness does not manifest itself in the same way across various nation states. Due to the variety of citizenship, migration, welfare and gender regimes across the continent, some states are more open and receptive than others in terms of making political claims based on race and/or intersectionality. Indeed, as we discussed in Chapter One, Britain and France's differing citizenship regimes deriving from their particular colonial histories mean that race is a more available category of expression and reception in Britain than in France (although this space in England is rapidly degrading in light of the backlash against multiculturalism and the 2016 Brexit vote).

However, in this chapter, we are concerned with the 'idea of Europe' and the theories and practices that constitute its (re)production. By examining Europe as an idealised space that was willed into being through its exploitative colonial relations and its attendant political and social theories, we can analyse the racial logic of Europe and consider why and how this logic is deployed in contemporary mythmaking of – and about – Europe.

So, what *is* Europe? In the hegemonic constructions of Europe in the Enlightenment theories of philosophers such as Immanuel Kant, Jean-Jacques Rousseau and John Locke, Europe is the expression of modernity. The typical telling of this familiar story is as follows: all men are equally endowed with rationality and logic. These rational men also have inalienable natural rights with which no actor can interfere. Thus, all rational men must enjoy liberty. These rational men are not subject to the arbitrary power of the state or the church, and it is only through a social contract between free men and the state that they voluntarily relinquish some of their liberty for the benefits of living in a society and enjoying the protection of a sovereign ruler. It is in the Enlightenment philosophies that we see the birth of modernity in the expression of the idea of the individual, rationality, equality and liberty. The question, of course, is how these philosophers define who gets included in the category of 'men' and who gets to enjoy the categorisation of being a rational individual who has inalienable rights to liberty and equality. In other words, who gets included and who gets excluded from European modernity?

As has been extensively documented by the Enlightenment philosophers themselves, the category of rational, free and equal men is exclusive. As Charles Mills (1997: 14) reminds us, 'race is in no way an "afterthought", a deviation from ostensibly raceless Western ideals, but rather a central shaping constituent of these ideals'. Infamously, although this is explained away or elided in contemporary interpretations, women, 'savages', slaves and indigenous peoples were excluded from modernity through the prevailing racial science as inherently irrational beings. Savages – or the colonial other: the Native or Aboriginal peoples, the African, the Indian, the slave – in particular were constructed as subhuman, incapable of logical reasoning and thus not subject to the equality or liberty enjoyed by 'men'. It is here, in the hierarchical binaries of modernity, that we can understand what Europe really is and what role race plays in the constitution of Europe. As Barnor Hesse (2007: 643) argues, 'modernity is racial'. To construct an identity of 'rational men' requires binary opposites in the shape of 'savages' or '(white) women'.[1] Thus, the idea of Europe is brought into being and is wholly dependent on its colonial entanglements and its particular patriarchal relations – which Europe, in turn, imposed on its colonial subjects (Hesse 2007; Lugones 2010; Delphy 2015a; Bhambra 2016).

We should also note the political economy of colonialism and the Enlightenment philosophies. To enslave and plunder necessitates the dehumanisation of the Other – and capitalist logic requires the exploitation and expropriation of the colonial subject's labour (Robinson 1983; Mills 1997). We would do well to remember that key Enlightenment theorists had a financial stake in imperial conquest, and their philosophies were put to work to justify their material interests.[2] As a result, we can see how colonialism was intellectualised and how colonialism made the Enlightenment – and hence European modernity – possible.

Once we understand that Europe is constituted by a racial logic of exclusion, violence and exploitation, we can identify how it functions on the basis of a racial contract. Following Charles Mills (1997: 12-13), a racial contract 'is not a contract between everybody (we the people) but just between the people who count, the people who really are the people (we the white people)'. Minority groups 'are objects rather than subjects of the agreement'. A racial contract establishes a racial polity, in which white supremacy is maintained through the defence of racial hierarchy. By constructing and justifying the racial order, white economic advantage and social power are institutionalised.

However, if the idea of Europe is constituted by race and the racial contract, how does the European polity (re)produce political racelessness, and what are the consequences for minority women? It is to this conundrum that we now turn.

Manufacturing white ignorance and white innocence

As we argued earlier, modernity is about knowledge production and the constitution of colonial identities: it is an epistemology of white supremacy and a justification of colonial conquest and plunder. Modernity and the unequal and exploitative political and social arrangements that follow from it are legitimated through a particular way of seeing and understanding the world. Mills (2007) calls this 'white ignorance', while Gloria Wekker (2016) names this as 'white innocence'. Part of the process of enforcement of the racial contract and maintaining the racial order is an agreement, explicit or tacit, among white people to 'misinterpret the world. One has to learn to see the world wrongly but with the assurances that this set of mistaken perceptions will be validated by the white epistemic authority, whether religious or secular' (Mills 1997: 18).

White ignorance and innocence are produced through a process of denial and forgetting. Even though colonialism and the invention of race play a central role in defining what Europe and modernity are, Europe's blood-soaked history of empire is expunged from the hegemonic understandings of itself, and the legacies of colonial conquest are erased from Europe's collective memory (Wekker 2016). Through the careful management of its official history and memory, Europe can represent itself, without irony, as a beacon of liberalism, tolerance and freedom, while never having to confront its colonial legacies in the form of institutionalised racism and state violence against minority groups. Consequently, white ignorance and innocence are an epistemology of ahistoricism. By selecting those parts of its history to valorise and those to forget, this undermines the various racial justice claims made by minority groups. Political racelessness is achieved by a calculated collective forgetting that subverts any claims for reparations for slavery and colonialism and renders inaudible any claims for positive action to tackle contemporary racial inequality and injustice. Political racelessness, in service to the racial contract, is a power relation to maintain white supremacy.

What makes the racial contract endure and political racelessness hard to counter is that it is enforced by both the European Right and Left. For minority women, this creates a monumental – but not impossible – barrier to the advancement of their political claims. It is to these issues that we will now turn.

Minority women and the epistemic violence of political racelessness

On the political Right, we should not be surprised that these actors enforce the racial contract through political racelessness. Seeking to conserve and defend the myths and traditions of a social order of exclusion is part of conservatism as a political ideology and practice. What is perhaps more surprising is how the political Left plays an active role in the maintenance of political racelessness, given the European Left's long and storied history of anti-racist and anti-fascist resistance. However, to understand the Left's role in political racelessness, we must analyse how the Left does not sit outside the strictures of the racial contract but plays a key role in its reproduction. The Left's dangerous myths about itself – that its movements for liberation are open and inclusive for all marginalised groups – are jealously protected. In order for the Left to defend its colonial identities it must deny that its conceptions of emancipatory politics are premised on, and made possible by, the effective exclusion of particular social groups who exist at the intersection of race, class, gender, sexuality, disability and legal status.

For instance, the systematic exclusion of minority women in many European feminist spaces is neither an 'unforeseen' nor an 'unfortunate' outcome of feminist theory and practice. Rather, it is crucial to understand how minority women's erasure is a central feature of the racial contract. In order for white feminism to maintain its fiction of universality – the default whiteness of the category of 'women' and the homogeneity of 'women's interests' – the wholesale exclusion of minority women is required. Furthermore, to secure the hegemonic whiteness of 'women' necessitates constructing minority women as either passive objects to be saved from their 'ethnic victimhood' or as alien Others who are irrelevant and a threat to the European polity. Under white feminism, it is doubtful whether minority women are women at all.

We can see these issues at play in the white feminist debates about the French state's 2004 law banning headscarves in public spaces. As Christine Delphy (2015a: 160) notes, white French feminists see 'these women [of immigrant backgrounds] through a filter of "otherness"' and as 'colonial subjects', 'making any empathy or identification with them impossible'. In Chapters Four and Five, we will discuss in the further detail how some of the white French participants in our study deploy a deeply damaging and counterproductive identity of 'victimhood' in order to advocate on behalf of minority women's claims, which is endorsed and reproduced by some minority women.

White feminism does not oppose the racial contract but, instead, is a key constituent element of it. Feminism is implicated in the racial contract, given the exclusionary systems of 'logic' that constitute the idea of Europe. Because patriarchy is an important stratifying element of modernity, for white women to secure (albeit partial) recognition and inclusion in European public spaces, requires the construction of Others who are illogical, irrational and barbaric.

Again, we also see these issues at play in the aftermath of the sexual assaults outside Cologne's main railway station on New Year's Eve in 2015. Some white German feminists – with the help of far-right groups – attempted to racialise sexual violence, by seemingly equating sexual assaults with the presence of Syrian refugees in the city. 'White women' were at risk in public spaces because of alien 'non-white Others'. (For excellent reporting on this, see Moore 2016.) A statement in the aftermath of the attacks demonstrates clearly the racial logic deployed by the European Women's Lobby, the largest umbrella organisation of women's group in the European Union that works to promote women's rights and gender equality:

> We demand an intensified search for the perpetrators and their severest punishment. The state, especially the police, is obliged to prevent attacks on women in the public space and to protect them accordingly. Sexual violence is not 'collateral damage' of street robbery or other crimes. Women are not fair game, and the Dome place in Cologne is not Tahrir place in Cairo. (European Women's Lobby 2016)

Note how a hierarchical binary is constructed between Cologne/Cairo, to demonstrate how civilised and rational Germany is in relation to an exotic, dangerous and barbaric Egypt. Cologne is not like Cairo, where, presumably, Egyptian women can be assaulted without consequence. White German women will not stand for such treatment. Even though the vast majority of migrants who entered Germany in the summer of 2016 were from Syria, we can see how events in a completely different country (mass sexual assaults in Tahrir Square during the Arab Spring and the fall of the dictator, Honsi Mubarak), can be weaponised to collectively implicate and condemn Syrian refugees. This is white ignorance, par excellence.

What is interesting to note about this affair is that under German law, the Cologne sexual assaults are technically not illegal. We are, of course, not in any way excusing violence against women, but it is interesting how the German state does not mandate consent from women being groped in public spaces but that this law, which institutionalises men's control over women's bodies, escaped the ire of some white feminists in the aftermath of the attacks (see Moore 2016 for details). Through the epistemological violence of erasure and misrecognition, minority women play a paradoxically essential role in maintaining the racial order ('they may be assaulted over there') by making possible white women's claims and access to public space ('we will not tolerate such treatment here').

We also see some parts of the white socialist and social democratic Left defend the racial order through attempts to secure an essentialised identity of the 'working class' and supposedly universal tenets such as 'class struggle'. There is a longstanding white socialist critique of feminism, anti-racism and LGBTQ recognition struggles on the basis that these analyses and resistances do not pay sufficient attention to the material conditions of class and fracture the Left through the practice of identity politics (Rowbotham et al 1979; Connolly 1991; Bock and James 1992; Hobsbawn 1996). Without the ability to speak in universalist terms, a coalition of the Left is impossible. As Todd Gitlin, a prominent left-wing critic of identity politics, has argued:

> Between Left and Right there has taken place a curious reversal. The Left believed in a common human condition, the Right in fundamental differences among classes, nations, races … Today it is the Right that speaks a language of commonalities. Its rhetoric of global markets and global freedoms has something of the old universalist ring. To be on the Left, meanwhile, is to doubt that one can speak of humanity at all. (Gitlin 1995: 84)

Some white socialists argue that counteracting the destructive effects of neoliberalism requires Left unity through a shared analysis of social problems emanating from economic inequality and class exploitation and a shared identity based on class conditions. We name this practice 'exclusionary universalism', as it seeks to erase race, gender, sexuality, disability and legal status for the sake of a false unity based solely on class.

Connected to this, and in light of the 2008 economic crisis and subsequent austerity measures, we have seen left-wing anti-austerity movements – from Occupy in Britain to *Los Indignados* in Spain and Greece to *Nuit Debout* in France – informed and inspired by economic populist theories and strategies (see, for example, Laclau 2005; Standing 2011). Margaret Canovan (1999: 3) defines populism as the 'appeal to "the people" against both the established structure of power and the dominant ideas and values of the society'. She argues that populism is a three-pronged concept: it is an articulation of popular grievances, a unifying call to the sovereign people and a challenge to perceived elite power and influence.[3] Populism gives actors the opportunity to reflect and re-interpret a generalised 'mood' of angst about 'politics as usual' and a means by which to disrupt the taken-for-granted ways in which power is exercised by both elite actors and institutions (Canovan 1999: 6). Populist politics rely on an essentialised and homogenised construction of 'the people' against the 'elites', which is hostile to – and seeks to displace – specific racial and gender justice claims. As Emejulu notes:

> Because feminism [and anti-racism] seek to transform the relationships, identities and values associated with 'women' and 'men' this is constructed by the progressive populist discourse as a 'special interest' that will split and undermine populists' hard won work of building the unity and solidarity of the people. (Emejulu 2011: 135)

On both the white socialist Left and the populist Left we can see the racial logic at work in insidious ways. Rather than take seriously the dynamics of racialisation (inflected by gender inequalities and legal status) in understanding social and economic inequality across different social groups, this complexity is denied and erased for the sake of a false unity of the 'working class' or 'the people' – the practice of exclusionary universalism. For example, in their analysis of Occupy, the Left populist movement which emerged in 2011 in response to the economic crisis and the inequality gap between the 99% ('the people') and the 1% ('the elites'), Maiguascha et al find that:

> Gender oppression is not central to either [Occupy's] diagnosis of the problem [of economic inequality] or its prescription for a better society ... If one is looking

for explicit recognition of gender oppression, as well as racism, ableism and other forms of discrimination based on ethnicity, language, religious affiliation, one has to examine the 'Safer Spaces Policy' … Here we do find reference to 'sexism' as well as 'homophobia', but these are presented as instances of disrespectful behaviour in the context of collective discussions and guarding against them as a matter of personal responsibility and a sensitive use of language. While the policy is certainly to be applauded, it in no way addresses 'sexism' as a structural power relation that operates beyond an individual's intentional actions. (Maiguascha et al 2016: 17-18)

Here we can see how racial and gender justice are downgraded and de-prioritised as merely ideal interpersonal interactions but not central to organising a Left populist political identity nor collective action. However, note that Maiguascha et al (2016) do find limited instances of intersectional understandings of austerity and politics.

Minority women pay a high price for the operation of white ignorance on the Left. Their intersectional social justice claims are not only misrecognised, they are also deemed a dangerous threat to the unity and coherence of left-wing politics and must be discounted. In Chapters Four and Five, we discuss in detail how our minority women activist participants negotiate this white ignorance in left-wing anti-austerity protest spaces.

Thus, we can see how political racelessness is epistemic violence that expels minority women from ostensibly progressive and radical spaces for social change. Minority women advancing political claims based on race, class and gender – and their intersections, within and beyond this trinity – cannot be heard and their particular views must be ignored epistemologically and empirically by many parts of the white socialist, social democratic, feminist and populist Left. In order to be 'included' in spaces predicated on their irrelevance, minority women must censor and efface themselves. What, then, does justice or solidarity mean in dominant left-wing politics, if it cannot support and sustain an intersectional politics?

Our view is that it is not the job of minority women to fix these problems with Left theories and political practices, nor to seek inclusion in spaces and movements that misrecognise them. Rather, we think there is much work to do in developing counternarratives, epistemologies and practices that legitimise and authorise minority women, their interests and claims. It is this issue that we will now explore.

Minority women and epistemic justice

To recognise minority women as intellectuals, political agents and authors of their lives requires purported 'allies' to critically consider why their chosen ideologies of gender, class, sexuality or disability will not permit complex understandings of race alongside – not in competition with – these other axes of difference. To counter the epistemic violence against minority women in the European polity requires a commitment to the dismantling of the identities, ideologies and social relations that legitimise and reproduce minority women's effacement. In other words, there is a need to take seriously Black feminism as both a process of knowledge production and of collective action for social justice (Lorde 1984; Mirza 1997; Sudbury 1998; Hill Collins 2000; Wekker 2016).

Minority women are differently positioned in institutional structures by virtue of their race, ethnicity, class, gender, sexuality, disability, language use and citizenship status – as we discuss further in Chapter Three. Solidarity requires minority women to resist essentialised notions of race and gender, and to recognise the differentials in power and privilege that exist between different kinds of women. Thus, while 'minority women' or 'women of colour' is an important identifier, it is only a starting point: we think that theorists and activists must seek to problematise this collective identity in order to name particular interests, inequalities and demands and to understand their contradictions across Europe.

By collectively struggling to understand these differing experiences, it becomes possible to recognise one's own positionality, which can spark solidarity, premised not on a false idea of homogeneity, as some on the white Left seek to advance, but on the shared knowledge of each other that the recognition of difference demands. In other words, difference is not the enemy of solidarity but the foundation for building a collective identity and a politics based on dignity and respect.

There is a need for knowledge production about the diverse, contradictory and competing notions of what it might mean to be a minority woman in Europe. There is also a need for dialogue: speaking with and listening to each other – especially to those women who are too often deliberately unheard – in order to develop knowledge and ideas for rethinking equality, freedom and solidarity (see Bassel (forthcoming 2017) on listening as a micropolitical process). Throughout the rest of our book, we seek to give space to the perspectives and experiences of a selection of minority women, in order to share their knowledge about their experiences of – and resistances to – austerity and their calculated erasure in Britain and France.

We do not seek to represent Black feminist knowledge production or resistance as 'new', but it is certainly dangerous and subversive to European modernity. We cannot recount here and do justice to the diversity of praxis in relation to Black feminism, but we would like to highlight one key element that is crucial in relation to legitimising and authorising minority women as actors and agents: lived experience.

Lived experience

By 'lived experience' we mean the knowledge acquired and produced through living life and the collective understandings and resistances that arise from being constructed as a subordinate and alien Other. As Patricia Hill Collins argues:

> Living life as Black women requires wisdom because knowledge about the dynamics of intersecting oppressions has been essential to ... Black women's survival ... Black women cannot afford to be fools of any type for our objectification as the Other denies us protections that white skin, maleness and wealth confer. (Hill Collins 2000: 257)

Centring the lived experiences of minority women is radical politics, because these experiences are denied and erased in both European social theory and political practice. Focusing on lived experience recuperates and makes minority women visible political actors in a context that asserts their passivity, absence and/or irrelevance. Insisting on minority women's lived experience is also a process of epistemic justice. We do not think that epistemic justice is necessarily about testimony or hermeneutics, as Miranda Fricker defines it:

> Testimonial justice is such that the hearer corrects for any influence of prejudice by re-inflating credibility to non-prejudiced levels; and hermeneutical justice is such that the hearer corrects for any influence of structural prejudice in social-interpretive resources by adjusting credibility levels appropriately to the hermeneutical handicap incurred by the speaker. (Fricker 2008: 70)

As we discussed earlier in this chapter, minority women's erasure and inaudibility are calculated and a central feature of European modernity, not an unfortunate and unforeseen consequence of it. Thus, focusing on the processes by which minority women can be heard and made credible seems to misunderstand the project of domination and exploitation of white supremacy. Rather, we are of the view that epistemic justice is about minority women producing counter-hegemonic knowledges for and about themselves. It is only by breaking away from the destructive hierarchical binaries of European modernity that minority women can authorise and legitimise themselves. We do not think that freedom and equality for minority women is possible under the current conditions of the European racial contract. Partial, contingent and grudging tolerance and inclusion can only be achieved for some groups that are deemed acceptable to the prevailing racial order.

However, we think that it is only when minority women assert control over how they are defined, what their experiences mean to them and how they might collectively imagine radical new futures – beyond the constraints of European modernity – that epistemic justice is achieved. Rather than starting with social theories that were constructed to dehumanise and debase them, we think lived experience is a necessary starting point from which to produce knowledge about the world as it is and how it *could be*.

Certainly, we do not wish to reproduce problematic essentialised identities in relation to lived experience. As we discussed earlier, lived experience, by its very nature, is diverse and varies greatly across individuals, groups and contexts. This is why lived experience is always relational – it relies on agency, recognition and dialogue between different kinds of minority women to construct shared meanings and take collective action. It is through collective understandings and resistances learned through lived experiences that political racelessness might be subverted. In this book, we attempt to examine how minority women understand their lived experiences under austerity and how these perceptions problematise the dominant ways of knowing and resisting austerity measures in France and Britain.

Conclusions

In this chapter, we have examined the disabling social theories of European modernity that have given rise to political racelessness. We have explored the racial logic of modernity and how white supremacy and domination are the key organising principles of Europe. We have also explored how political racelessness is made possible through an epistemology of white ignorance and white innocence, which allows Europe to forget and expunge its colonial brutalities from its collective memory and senses of self. Political racelessness, we have argued, is a form of epistemic violence that minority women must confront and counter. Rather than being excepted from the logic of white supremacy, we also demonstrated how aspects of left-wing politics actively participate in maintaining the racial order. To achieve epistemic justice, we assert that understanding and theorising the lived experiences of minority women is the crucial first step. Centring the lived experiences of minority women is disruptive to the racial logic of Europe, because it exposes and subverts the idea of minority women as passive, irrelevant objects to be acted upon by white agents. Focusing on lived experiences is also a counter-hegemonic process of producing knowledge for the benefit of minority women. In this way, it is possible to imagine radical futures beyond the confines of European modernity.

We will now explore the lived experiences of minority women under the austerity regimes in France and Britain in further detail, and demonstrate how Europe's dominant ideas of economic inequality and precarity are destabilised when we centre the experiences of this diverse group of women.

Notes

[1]   It is important to note that women of colour are almost completely erased in these binaries but are brought sharply back into focus when white women seek to assert their humanity and inclusion in public spaces through the dehumanisation of 'non-European' men and women from Mary Wollstonecraft to Simone de Beauvoir to Hannah Arendt. We will demonstrate this in our discussion about the operation of white feminism.

[2]   John Locke, for example, was a large plantation investor in America.

[3]   This appears in Emejulu (2011).

THREE

Whose crisis counts?

Introduction

In this chapter, we examine in detail minority women's institutionalised precarity in pre- and post-crisis France, England and Scotland. Even though minority women experience systemic social and economic inequalities, too often their experiences are erased or devalued by social movement allies and policy makers alike. This is political racelessness enacted through both political discourse and empirical data gathering and analysis.

We argue that minority women experience a paradox of misrecognition – they are simultaneously invisible and hypervisible in the constructions of poverty, the economic crisis and austerity. As Heidi Mirza (2015: 4) notes, minority women are caught between what Ann Phoenix has termed 'normative absence and pathological presence' (Phoenix 1987) in how we think about social problems and policy interventions. Using an intersectional framework, we will demonstrate how minority women, a heterogeneous group, experience systematic discrimination and multidimensional inequalities based on their race, class, gender and legal status. In this chapter, we focus specifically on minority women's experiences in the labour market, as access to the labour market and the quality of available work is a key determinant of poverty and inequality. We also explore the particular ways in which minority women are rendered either invisible or hypervisible in key social policies meant to address their routinised inequalities.

The countries examined in this book are case studies, which differ in relation to the gender patterns of work and care. France is often placed under the category of 'continental' model of welfare state (Eydoux 2014: 154). According to different authors who focus primarily on the effects of the economic crisis on gender equality in France, the policies implemented as a response tended to 'reinforce the traditional male (main) breadwinner model' (Eydoux 2014: 155; see also Smith and Villa 2014). Britain, in contrast, is characterised as a 'liberal welfare state', closer in resemblance to the United States than its European neighbours because of its relatively minimalist approach to provision, which focuses more on means-tested social welfare than on universal programmes (Esping-Andersen 1990, 1999; Clarke and Newman 1997).

Our intention in this chapter is to provide the context for the activism by and with minority women in our subsequent chapters. Our intention is not comparative and we therefore do not aim for a perfect empirical match; instead, we wish to provide the reader with tools to better understand the shape and the scope of minority women's activism in each context.

Minority women and routinised precarity

Even before the 2008 economic crisis, minority ethnic groups and minority women in particular in Britain were experiencing persistent economic and social hardships.

Labour markets

The high rates of poverty and inequality for minority groups are directly linked to their experiences of, and relationships to, the labour markets in each country. Regardless of educational outcomes, minority groups are more likely than their white counterparts to be unemployed or underemployed (Emejulu 2008; Bassel 2012).

In an inquiry into the labour market experiences of Black, Pakistani and Bangladeshi women in Britain, conducted on behalf of the All Party Parliamentary Group for Race and Community (APPG) for the July–November 2012 period, Vicky Butler (2012) notes that: '[f] or all groups except for Indian men, ethnic minority unemployment has consistently remained higher than the rate for white people since records began'. In Britain, Black women (this includes both African and Caribbean women) have an unemployment rate of 17.7%, for Pakistani and Bangladeshi women it is 20.5% compared to 6.8% for white women. This post-crisis analysis demonstrates the longstanding legacy of *pre-crisis* inequality for minority women: consistently higher unemployment since records began.

For those minority women and men in the labour market, they must negotiate a so-called 'ethnic penalty' that depresses wages and concentrates them in low-paid, temporary and unstable work (Butler 2012). Minority women, of course, must negotiate both an ethnic *and* a gender penalty that over-concentrates them in low-skilled, low-paid and insecure work. Importantly, in Scotland and England, minority ethnic young people leave school with better qualifications and are more likely to go to university than their white counterparts, but they do not reap the benefits of their qualifications in terms of labour market outcomes (Butler 2012; Crawford and Greaves 2015; Kamenou et al 2013).

France does not consistently collect or disaggregate its socioeconomic data by race or ethnicity, making it extremely difficult to capture variations between different minority groups (Simon 2007, 2008a, 2008b, 2010, 2012; Tin 2015; Fassin 2015; Faure and Vécrin 2015).[1] 'Place of birth' is used as a proxy for race and ethnicity, which masks racial disparities (Sabbagh and Peer 2008: 3). Unhelpfully, French-born, second- and third-generation minority groups are clustered under the homogenised category 'of immigrant origin' which, in itself, reveals how Black and Brown French citizens are constructed as alien Others, who exist outside the French polity.[2] The category of 'migrant' is a shorthand for the experiences of many different racial and ethnic groups: European and non-European immigrants. Problems arise with the category of 'non-migrant', where French citizens of colour get included but their unequal outcomes are masked because statistics are not consistently disaggregated by race and ethnicity. These categories are themselves unstable, because sometimes French citizens of colour are included in both 'migrant' and 'non-migrant' categories. This is political racelessness as official state policy. Mapping the confusing statistical landscape is beyond the scope of this book, but it is important to understand how these statistical categories reflect France's (unacknowledged) ongoing colonial entanglements and the memory of the Vichy regime (Simon 2008a, 2008b). As we will demonstrate throughout the rest of this book, the category 'of immigrant origin' is activated in particular ways, both explicit and implicit, to deny or undermine minority women activists' social justice claims in France.

In terms of minority groups' labour market experiences, we see a similar pattern in France: members of visible ethnic minorities from Sub-Saharan Africa, Turkey and the Maghreb are more likely to be unemployed or underemployed with respect to the white population (Meurs and Pailhé 2008, 88, 95; Algan et al 2010, F24; Brinbaum and Guégnard 2012, 62; Minni and Okba 2014, 7). In France, one measure of the unemployment rate for French 'minority' groups is about 17% compared to 11% to the white French 'majority' (Gobillon et al 2014: 110).[3] However, using another measure, 'immigrant' men have an unemployment rate of 11.9% and 'immigrant' women of 15.1% in comparison to unemployment rates of 'native born' men of 7.2% and 'native born' women of 7.7% (OECD 2010).

Furthermore, when employed, members of visible minority groups tend to be concentrated in temporary employment and earn significantly less than white individuals with comparable educational achievements (Algan et al 2010, F17–F19; Minni and Okba 2014, 8). In contrast to Scotland and England, women and men who belong to visible minority groups must also cope with poorer educational outcomes vis-à-vis their white counterparts (Felouzis 2003, 437; Meurs and Pailhé 2008, 95; Brinbaum and Kieffer 2009, 563; Algan et al 2010, F13–F14; Minni and Okba 2014, 2). According to the Insee *enquêtes Emploi* (Employment Survey) (Insee, 2007), the unemployment rate of immigrant women and men residing in the *zones urbaines sensibles* (ZUS) is on average 28% and 22% respectively (Okba 2009: 4).[4]

Although minority women tend to have better qualifications in comparison to their male counterparts, they struggle to capitalise on their educational advantage in the labour market (Meurs and Pailhé 2008, 89, 103ff; Brinbaum and Kieffer 2009, 595; Meurs and Pailhé 2010, 136; Brinbaum and Guégnard 2012, 63). Similarly to what occurs in England and Scotland, minority women workers in France are overconcentrated in low-skilled, low-paid and temporary employment (Frickey and Primon 2006; Meurs and Pailhé 2008, 96–7, 101; Chrisafis 2011; Brinbaum and Guégnard 2012, 63; Minni and Okba 2014, 7).

Minority groups' precarity in the labour market in all three cases is due to a number of factors:

- First, and most important, is the institutionalised racial and gender discrimination that minority women and men face which disadvantages them in interviews and selection, promotion, professional development, redundancy and firing processes. As has been well documented, job searching while Black or Brown means that minority candidates with similar or better qualifications than their white counterparts are less likely to be interviewed, to be hired or to secure equal pay (OECD 2008; Kamenou et al 2013; Bunel et al 2016).
- Second, minority groups, particularly migrants, are less likely to have their overseas qualifications and professional experience recognised in Scotland, England or France, thus hindering their labour market participation from the outset (Al Ariss and Özbilgin 2010, 279; Zikic et al 2010; Butler 2012; Netto et al 2015, 515, 517).
- Finally, in all three countries, there is a problem of the spatial mismatch between where permanent, well-paid jobs are located and where minority groups tend to reside, creating an additional barrier to accessing available employment opportunities. In general, minority ethnic groups live in areas with higher unemployment (Patacchini and Zenou 2005; L'Horty and Sari 2008; Pan Ké Shon

2009; Maxwell 2010; Meurs and Pailhé 2010, 139-40; Butler 2012; Algava and Lhommeau 2013, 22; Gobillon et al 2014).

Poverty

In pre-crisis Britain, the poverty rate for minority groups was 40%, double the rate of the white population (Kenway and Palmer 2007; Platt 2007). There are considerable variations of poverty between minority ethnic groups, with Bangladeshi, Pakistani and Black African groups faring the worst (about 70% of Bangladeshi children are growing up poor) and Indian, Chinese and Black Caribbean groups faring better (Indian and Chinese groups, in particular, are more likely to be educated to degree level and be in professional employment). These differences in outcomes are attributable to a number of factors, including the differing labour market participation of women, household size and composition, and residential locations (Kenway and Palmer 2007).

While robust ethnic statistics are collected in Britain, they are often situated in parallel to gender statistics, making 'intersectional' monitoring challenging. As the All Party Parliamentary Group on Race and Community report notes, monitoring by 'dual characteristics' of gender and ethnicity is not required under the Equality Act 2010 or its guidance, and is not addressed under the Equality and Human Rights Commission's statutory code on employment (Butler 2012: 11). These data are also hard to access, unevenly collected and difficult for a layperson to comprehend. Initiatives like the Runnymede Trust's 'Race Equalities Scorecard' attempt to improve access and action in relation to equality statistics.[5]

In pre-crisis France, 21% of descendants of immigrants are poor,[6] in comparison to 10.6% of the white French population (Lombardo and Pujol 2011: 78). The poverty rate of migrant households and mixed households varies considerably according to the geographic origins of the migrants: African migrant households (that is, Black and Arab/ Berber ethnic minorities) are characterised by a much higher poverty rate with respect to their white European counterparts, about 43% and 24% respectively. A similar pattern is found when comparing mixed households: the poverty rate is approximately 27% for mixed households when the person of reference is an African migrant compared to about 11% for European mixed households (Lombardo and Pujol 2010).

Constructing minority groups as alien Others

Twinned with these persistently economically hard times for minority groups are the construction of particular intersections of race, ethnicity, religion and gender as 'problematic' in political and policy debates (Hancock 2004). Minority groups' experiences do not feature prominently nor inform discussions of policy problems or solutions, unless groups are interpellated in particularly racialised and gendered discussions of social problems (Phoenix and Phoenix 2012). Here we see how minority groups are simultaneously invisible and hypervisible in debates about poverty, unemployment and inequality. Here we also see the paradoxes of political racelessness used to reinforce the racial contract. For instance, the 'public issue' of minority unemployment often only features in public and policy debate when linked to periods of urban unrest, such as the 2005 French Paris riots or the 2011 English riots. Minority groups' persistent poverty and unemployment is typically only highlighted as a 'public issue' in the contexts of moral panics in each country about 'failed' state strategies, whether in relation to multiculturalist policies (in Britain) or assimilationist policies (in France).

For example, in reaction to the 2011 English riots, Professor David Starkey opined on BBC2's flagship news and current affairs programme *Newsnight* that a 'Jamaican patois' had intruded upon English cities, transforming these places into foreign territories (Phoenix and Phoenix 2012: 62). For Starkey, deviant 'black culture' is contagious and has been adopted by some white, working-class people, who he refers to with the pejorative label of 'chavs' to argue: 'what has happened is that a substantial section of the chavs have become black. The whites have become black' (Phoenix and Phoenix 2012: 100). As Phoenix and Phoenix argue, Starkey's explanation is intersectional, 'bringing together racialisation, gender and (implicitly) social class' but always to pathologise Blackness without addressing underlying social and economic and political causes – the public issues – of the riots (Phoenix and Phoenix 2012: 64-5). Thus, routinised unemployment and poverty are defined as the private problem of the racialised poor and only become a public issue when the everyday social order is disrupted.

For women in particular, the routinised crisis of poverty is privatised and is only defined as a public issue when their 'failed femininities' lead to family breakdown and public disorder (Allen and Taylor 2012a, 2012b). The 'troubled mothers' and 'failing riot girls' of the August 2011 riots in England embody the:

[longstanding] condemnation of young working-class women but in a new context. The gendering of the riots tells us many things, but perhaps most importantly that classed and racialised distinctions and boundaries of failed and ideal femininities are becoming more accentuated under the coalition government and its austerity policies. (Allen and Taylor 2012a)

Thus, we can see how racialised women and men are delicately balanced between 'normative absence and pathological presence' (Phoenix 1987) and how this shapes both our understanding of social problems and the public and policy debates about possible policy interventions.

In France, we see similar issues at play in terms of racialised groups' invisibility and hypervisibility. A few months before the November 2005 riots, which began in the eastern suburbs of Paris and quickly spread throughout the country, the then Interior Minister, Nicolas Sarkozy, branded groups of youths in the Parisian suburbs as *racaille* [scum], and vowed to clean them out with a *Kärcher*, the brand name of a high-powered water cannon (Canet et al 2015; Ireland 2005; Lannelongue 2015; Pulham 2005). Importantly, former President Sarkozy persisted in using the term *racaille* to describe the mainly Black and Arab/Berber rioters during the uprising and for years afterwards (Winter 2009, 271; Cheutin 2016). In this controversial statement, Sarkozy made visible the rift between *français de souche* (white, native-born French) and *français issues de l'immigration* (second-generation immigrant French). The deterioration of *les banlieues*, routine police brutality and the economic inequalities that French people of colour experience are regarded as the private, invisible problems of the racialised poor. When the social order is disrupted, as we saw in 2005, French minorities become, in themselves, a hypervisible problem of the failures of assimilationist social policies (The Guardian 2005; Fassin 2015). The debates over the hijab, the burkini and halal food become key markers of anti-Frenchness and the policy of *laïcité* [secularism] is weaponised and used as a disciplining device to defend 'authentic Frenchness' from alien Others (Winter 2009; Bassel 2012; Delphy 2015b; Dremeaux 2016; L'Obs 2016; Shabi 2016).

Minority women's routinised crises

The economic and social disparities that minority groups face are hardly new, and we have not outlined anything particularly groundbreaking here for scholars of race and ethnicity. However, Dara Strolovitch (2013:

169-70) helpfully reminds us that 'it is not inevitable that a bad thing will be defined and treated as bad, much less that it will be regarded as a crisis'. She goes on to argue that, minority groups, 'are thus regarded ... as the perpetuators of their own crises which are attributable to individual defects or cultural dysfunctions'.

Thus what is important to remember when we think about minority groups and their crises of unemployment and poverty is that the very ordinariness of their experiences, combined with the construction of some racial, ethnic and gender intersections as problematic, serves to help to privatise the public issue of their persistent precarity. Lest we attribute the privatisation of public issues as a problem solely for minority groups, it is important to note how the experiences of white working-class men and boys, in particular the sharp declines in their educational and economic outcomes, are also classified as a private trouble of cultural dysfunction, brought on by the (unsubstantiated claim of) intergenerational transmission of fecklessness, low aspirations and a lack of self-responsibility (Jones 2011; MacDonald et al 2013; Tyler 2013).

Given that minority groups, and minority women in particular, were already in economic crisis before the 2008 global financial meltdown – but paradoxically were ignored and yet interpellated in deeply problematic ways during periods of social unrest – we, as researchers, are faced with a dilemma. Throughout our research project we have been constantly struck by the contradiction of examining phenomena that appeared to be 'new' but, when placed in the context of minority women's lives, these issues were, in fact, a sharpening and a prolongation of these women's ordinary and everyday experiences of inequality.

Minority women experience what we call 'routinised crises': persistent, institutionalised and ordinary hardships in everyday life. Their persistently high unemployment and poverty rates are not 'exceptional' and not necessarily problems to be addressed, since they are indicators of capitalism, patriarchy and white supremacy operating as intended. Once we understand minority women's precarity as the banality of everyday inequalities, we can begin to understand the politics of the construction of the 2008 economic crisis.

To be sure, world financial markets were on the brink of collapse, but the naming of the crisis and the specific groups assumed to be affected by the crisis is what interests us here. As Strolovitch (2013) persuasively argues, the naming of the 2008 crisis is a power relation that focuses policy attention and resources on the transformed economic landscape that the economically privileged must now negotiate. What the 2008 crisis signifies is that middle-class groups are being drawn into precarious social and economic circumstances, in which minority women have always had to struggle. That policy attention is now focused on the difficulty of securing a mortgage, the widespread introduction of zero-hours contracts, the decline in real wages and the hidden poverty and unemployment of those who are self-employed denotes the 'exceptional circumstances' in which the economically privileged groups find themselves. The problems of exploitative pay and conditions, insecure work and the barriers to building wealth have long been experienced by minority women, but what is 'new' is that middle-class groups' social protections are now being systematically eroded, so that they resemble (but are not identical to) minority women's precarious circumstances.

Consequently, we think there is a damaging bias embedded within the conception of the 2008 economic crisis and subsequent austerity measures that makes it extremely difficult to recognise and take action on minority women's intersecting inequalities. The very 'banality' of minority women's disadvantage, combined with the disrespectful and disparaging constructions of some minority women, exclude them from the European public sphere and undermine their efforts to build solidarity. It seems that the framing of the crisis is another instance of political racelessness. Centring minority women's routinised crises can help us to legitimise and make visible the particularities of their inequalities and can help to authorise their resistances.

We will now explore how minority women are affected by austerity measures in the aftermath of the 2008 economic crisis.

Minority women's routinised crises and austerity measures since 2008

As we argued in Chapter One, minority women are disproportionately disadvantaged by the economic crisis and the cuts in public spending because of their already existing precarity and because of their particular relationships with the social welfare states in Scotland, England and France. What is important to bear in mind is that the crises that minority women experience are not new, as such, but are a sharpening and deepening of their routinised crises that are largely ignored by social movement allies and policy makers. In this section, we focus on those changes to public sector employment, local government services and the benefits system, and situate minority women in relation to these changes in each country.

The shrinking public sector in England and Scotland

Cutting spending on the public sector is a double hazard for minority women, because they are more likely to work in this sector and are more likely to use public services (Women's Budget Group 2012; Sandhu et al 2013; Taylor-Gooby 2013; Emejulu and Bassel 2013; Emejulu and Bassel 2015). In Scotland and England, 34% of women and 16% men work in the public sector. Yet the proportion of women in the public sector varies among different minority groups: 45% of Black Caribbean women, 37% of Pakistani women, 36% of Bangladeshi, 33% of Black African women and 27% of Indian women work in this sector, compared to 34% of white women (Sandhu et al 2013: 10-11).

We see such large numbers of minority women working in the public sector for two reasons:

- First, the public sector encompasses a number of caring professions dominated by minority women, such as teaching, nursing and midwifery, social work and social care. Given the labour shortages after the Second World War and the recruitment of Black Caribbean, Indian and Pakistani workers to fill the gaps in a rapidly expanding public sector, these patterns of employment continue today.
- Second, the public sector has traditionally had lower barriers to entry because of the application of anti-discriminatory laws, codes and guidelines that allowed minority women successful entrée, unlike the private sector, into these jobs. Thus, cutting the public sector is cutting the lifeline to professional and unionised work for many minority women.

As Hastings et al (2015, 20) have found in England and Scotland, the unprecedented cuts to the public sector are taking place in a context of a 'rise in overall need and needs becoming more intense for the most vulnerable'. As the block grant to local government is cut, officials have been forced to make a number of unsustainable staffing changes that impact on minority women workers. Minority women must negotiate compulsory redundancies, increased workloads and, consequently, increases in stress and sickness, because they are unable to cope with the pressures of a transformed working environment.

What makes the cuts to local government so disturbing is that local government officials, in the first wave of austerity from 2011 to 2015, have already made efficiency savings by cutting backroom/middle management staff. Because the order of the cuts is so large, council leaders have to cut frontline/operational staff, specialist service staff (for example anti-violence against women workers) and those working in preventative services (such as youth work, community centres and social care). By cutting these positions, this is degrading the quality of services offered by local government (UNISON 2014; Imkaan 2015).

The declining quality of local government services matters, as Hastings et al (2015: 22) argue, because this residualisation has the long-term effect of making public services the 'services of last resort'. In other words, when the quality of services starts to decline, economically privileged groups will stop using local government services and these services will only be used by the very poorest with the most complex needs. As has been well documented, 'services for poor people tend to be poor services' – and highly vulnerable to further cuts (McCormick and Philo 1995). Thus, for those minority women working in the public sector, they face insecurity in their working lives in which their jobs, pay and conditions are under threat and the services they provide are underfunded or eliminated altogether.

The shrinking public sector in France

The French public sector is mainly composed of women (Marty 2015; Métral 2016). Conversely, in the private sector, there are fewer women in comparison to men. Similar to the situation in England and Scotland, reductions in public spending mainly impact women, because they form the majority in the public employment sector and they also rely more on public services (Marty 2015: 127). In 2007, the French government implemented the rule of '*non-remplacement*',[7] later abrogated in 2012, to reduce the budget on public spending by removing 150,000 public sector jobs in the period 2008-12 (Lafarge and Le Clainche 2010; Marty 2011, 8; Cours des comptes 2012; The Economist 2013; Marty 2015, 128).

In terms of access to public services, 'because of the decrease in social services and essential services such as children's centres, social work services, health and care services, women have to take on an important part of what is no longer covered by the state [*la collectivité*]' (Marty 2015: 128). Specifically, public services such as maternity services and abortion clinics have been reduced (Baillot and Evain 2012).

Again, because of the lack of disaggregated statistics, we cannot document how minority women public sector workers are being impacted by these cuts to state spending.

Austerity and access to public services in England and Scotland

Minority women who seek to access public services are also being disadvantaged by austerity measures. Because of the high poverty rates of minority women, this means that they are more likely to use public services, less likely to pay for private services and are disproportionately affected when public services are restructured. Furthermore, because minority women are more likely to be living in the poorest areas, their local councils are being hit hardest by austerity measures (Beatty and Fothergill 2013; Sandhu et al 2013; UNISON 2014; Hastings et al 2015; Neville 2016). Between 2010 and 2015, the central government grant to local authorities was cut by £11.3 billion (UNISON 2014: 3).

For the first tranche of austerity between 2010 and 2011, 'English local authorities cut spending by 27% in real terms, compared to 11% in Scotland' (Hastings et al 2015: 6). The most deprived local authorities in England have cut spending by £220 per head compared to £40 per head in the richest authorities. In Scotland, because of the Scottish Government's austerity mitigation plan, the cuts have been more evenly distributed across local councils, with a 5% decrease of spending for the richest areas and a 7% decrease for the poorest (Hastings et al 2015: 6). What is important to note in council leaders' decisions about cutting services is that not all services are affected in the same way. As a strategy, most councils have sought to protect 'pro-poor' services, such as social care, homelessness support and public transport. Consequently, other areas have been hit harder, such as museums and galleries, adult education, and environment and planning services (Hastings et al 2015: 17).

Even though councils in England and Scotland are trying to protect pro-poor services in a context of shrinking budgets, the quality of these services is still declining. Because of the pace of the cuts, councils have had to get creative in terms of shoring up their service provision. For example, many councils have centralised their services by closing satellite offices located in neighourhoods and instead have created multifunctional, 'one-stop shops' for their services in a single location. For other services, such as libraries, youth work and leisure centres, they have started charging for the use of access and/or have reduced the opening hours (UNISON 2014; Hastings et al 2015).

These changes to the quality and provision of services are having a devastating impact on minority groups, particularly women. For example, as local council services are centralised, this reduces access to them, since minority women are more likely to use public transport. Also, given that the public transport subsidy is being cut, this creates an additional barrier to accessing vital public services. As libraries and leisure centres start to charge and/or curtail their opening hours, this increases minority women's isolation as they are unable to socialise – and take a break from their children or adult relatives requiring care – in these once accessible spaces. Our focus group with first- and second-generation Chinese Scots in Glasgow echoed these concerns about increased isolation because of cuts to vital services. As one participant said:

> 'I feel sorry for the fact that all this [a local community service] is disappearing ... Where can they go? Where you can meet people? They get isolated ... there is [sic] not enough facilities.' (CRER Participant 1)

As the cuts to environmental services start to bite, we see the degrading of the local environment, in terms of the accumulation of litter and fly-tipping, particularly in the poorest neighbourhoods. Both Hastings et al (2015: 18-20) and UNISON (2014: 3-4) have documented how women, in particular, feel unsafe walking the streets or using local parks or community centres, because these are perceived to be poorly maintained and dangerous. Thus, minority women activists are faced with a real challenge of maintaining a public presence in a context that seeks to re-privatise them and their interests and needs.

In Scotland, England and France, the shrinking public sector also means that many of its services are being put out to competitive tender, to which both the private and third sectors bid. This tendering process has devastating consequences for the third sector and minority women activists in all three countries. We will discuss how austerity is transforming the third sector – and the impact that this has on minority women's activism – in greater detail in Chapter Four.

The changing benefits system in France

In France, as in other countries, additional benefits and one-off payments were used to sustain household consumption and to protect families' living standards in the aftermath of the 2008 economic crisis. These crisis measures had a positive impact on the net disposable income of beneficiaries (Marchal et al 2014: 15; Marty 2015: 127). For example, in 2009, the French government implemented measures aimed at reducing income taxes for low-income families, and it increased them from 2014 for better-off families with children (OECD 2014).

Moreover, between 2009 and 2011, a one-off increase in vouchers and easier access to benefits for lone parents were introduced. Also in 2009-10, France extended the reach of its unemployment insurance, by reducing the minimum amount of time of affiliation required to allow people to access unemployment benefits.[8] In France, the first phase of the crisis also saw family policies to help restart the economy through exceptional measures: beneficiaries were given housing and subsistence payments (Collombet and Hiltunen 2013).[9]

However, in reviewing these changes, some observers note that this increased access to benefits was only in place in the 'first phase' (the recession) following the crisis.[10] It is in the third phase (austerity) after 2011 – when France failed to achieve its the pre-crisis levels of production and the GDP growth rates fell to 0.2% in 2012, 0.7% in 2013 and again to 0.2% in 2014 – that the impacts on women are most significant. According to the Independent Annual Growth Survey (iAGS 2014), the main factor explaining this stagnation phase has been the so-called 'fiscal consolidation' policy. Under this umbrella concept are two important measures: increases in direct and indirect household taxes; and restrictions on public spending. It is due to the policy of fiscal consolidation that we see the widening of the gender gap in relation to household income.

From 2010, unemployment benefits were reduced and more stringent eligibility requirements were introduced, as occurred to various degrees in other European countries. The consolidation measures implemented in the third phase of the crisis (austerity) were mainly aimed at making savings on working-age transfers (such as unemployment, social assistance, disability and family benefits) (OECD 2014: 48). For example, while the contribution requirements for claiming unemployment benefits were reduced and the overall duration of unemployment benefit was slightly increased, the one-off payment, introduced in 2009, in favour of jobseekers who were not entitled to unemployment benefits, was eliminated. In this regard, the OECD report (2014: 129) shows a drop of 0.5 percentage points in the receipt rates of out-of-work benefits in the period 2007-10 for lone parents.

Furthermore, since 2010, stricter eligibility conditions and lower benefit levels targeted the old-age pensions in France (OECD 2014: 56).[11] Healthcare services were also hit by these fiscal consolidations. As a result of these measures, patients have needed to make larger out-of-pocket payments to access healthcare services. Although exemptions and caps could reduce the impact of these cuts on more vulnerable groups, it is recognised that these measures were particularly detrimental to low-income French households (OECD 2014: 58).

All in all, in contrast to what occurred in England and Scotland, public social expenditure in France increased in the period 2012-13 by 0.5% in comparison to the 2007-09 and 2009-10 periods (OECD 2014: 127). However, it is worth noting that France – along with other European countries like Italy, Greece, Portugal and Spain –spent more money on transfers to well-off families (that is, households in the top 30% of income) than to low-income families (that is, households in the bottom 30% of income) (OECD 2014: 61).

The changing benefits system in England and Scotland

In Britain, since minority women are more likely to be living in poverty, they, 'on average, receive a higher proportion of their income from working age benefits or tax credits' (Sandhu et al 2013). Consequently, Britain's unprecedented changes to the tax and benefit system disproportionately harm minority women's incomes and livelihoods. At the time of writing (September 2016), Sandhu et al (2013) have undertaken the only study exploring the cumulative and real-terms impact of the cuts to the benefits system on minority women in Britain. We will not repeat their important work here, but highlight some key changes that are having an outsize impact on minority women's incomes.

One of the most important changes in the benefits system that was helmed by the previous Work and Pensions Secretary, Iain Duncan Smith, is the reduction in housing benefit for tenants in both social housing and private rented accommodation. Since 2011, the local housing allowance has been slashed, so that it only covers rents up to the bottom 30% of rents locally. For tenants in private rented accommodation, particularly those who live in areas of high housing costs, this means that they will be forced to move to cheaper accommodation or to top up the shortfall in rent out of their own pockets. Given that minority groups are concentrated in London and that London is one of the most expensive cities on the planet for housing, this change to the local housing allowance means that many minority households will be forced to leave the city in search of lower rents (Sandhu et al 2013: 24). Thus, when some commentators talk of the 'vast social cleansing' of London of the poor, it is the effect of these kinds of benefit changes to which they refer (Taylor 2015).

For those tenants in social housing, the situation is also bleak. From 2013, the then Coalition government introduced the so-called 'bedroom tax': families that are assessed to be living in homes larger than their needs will have their housing benefit cut. They will face a

14% cut in housing benefit for the first under-occupied bedroom and a 25% cut for two or more bedrooms (Sandhu et al 2013: 24). Given that minority women tend to live in multigenerational households, unlike their white counterparts, this cut in benefits is having a significant impact on minority households and will increase overcrowding and stressful household situations and will force minority women to move away from their neighbourhoods.

The other key change in the benefits system that we wish to highlight in relation to minority women is the introduction of the benefit cap and the phasing in of Universal Credit. The benefit cap is the combined maximum amount of all the benefits that a working-age adult can receive in a given year. This includes housing benefit, jobseeker's allowance, child tax credits and income support, but excludes most of the benefits for people with disabilities. When it was first introduced in 2013, the cap was initially set at £26,000. However, from 2014, this cap has been cut to £23,000 for London residents and £20,000 for the rest of the country. At first glance, this cap seems generous. However, given the high housing costs, and given that most minority women live in London, many will struggle to make ends meet on this income. The cap translates as £500 per week for couples and single parents, regardless of how many children they have and £350 per week for single working-age adults with no children.

Universal Credit was the flagship policy of Duncan Smith at the Department for Work and Pensions. Following Duncan Smith's resignation in 2016, due to his involvement in the Brexit campaign, the fate of Universal Credit is uncertain. Nevertheless, at the time of writing, Universal Credit is a new means-tested benefit that will replace six current benefits for jobseekers. Universal Credit is meant to streamline the payment of benefits and also to calibrate them, so that benefits do not create disincentives for work. There is widespread agreement among welfare rights advocates and policy makers that a simplified system of claiming benefits that does not disadvantage jobseekers in the labour market is sorely needed. However, Universal Credit, currently in its pilot phase in London, actually *reduces* support for low-income households.

Even though the former Chancellor of the Exchequer, George Osborne, introduced a National Living Wage in 2016, any benefits that might be reaped from the National Living Wage are completely wiped out by the drastic cuts in support for the poorest households, especially lone parent households and households with more than two children where one parent is working part-time (Hirsch 2015). Given that minority women are living in the poorest households, are more likely to be unemployed or underemployed, and are more likely to be living in households with children, Universal Credit is likely to extend and deepen their precarity and insecurity.

Conclusions

In this chapter, we have attempted to explore in detail how minority women experience routinised crises – institutionalised, ordinary and everyday social and economic inequalities that are treated as unremarkable in policy and political discourses until minority groups disrupt the social order. Minority women are delicately balanced between invisibility and hypervisibilty in policy debates about inequality. This paradoxical position means that their particular interests and experiences of precarity are misrecognised and/or erased.

Rather than illuminating minority women's intersectional inequalities, the frame of the economic crisis reinforces political racelessness. We have demonstrated how, even before the 2008 economic crisis, minority women were experiencing high levels of poverty and disadvantage due to institutionalised discrimination in the labour market, which meant they are more likely to be unemployed or underemployed in comparison to their white counterparts. Because France does not collect statistics based on race, minority women's experiences in the labour market and in the benefits system are politically erased. Minority women's experiences in France have only been made visible through the skillful manoeuvring of some committed researchers and activists.

We have also discussed how the policy frame of the 2008 economic crisis actually further erases minority women's precarity, by focusing policy attention and resources on the exceptional experiences of the economically privileged at this uncertain economic moment in time. The 2008 economic crisis and subsequent austerity measures do not represent a fundamentally new experience of precarity for minority women; rather, this is a sharpening and deepening of their already existing inequalities. We argue that we must resist the temptation of using this policy frame as an explanation of minority women's inequalities, as this actually has the effect of erasing their experiences and of re-inscribing those of the economically privileged.

At the time writing (September 2016), mass protests – *Nuit Debout* – have erupted across France in response to proposed changes to its labour law [*loi travail*], bringing France 'closer' to Britain in weakening job protections and making trade union consultations expendable in negotiating working conditions. Also, following the shock Brexit vote in Britain, it appears that the British economy is in danger of entering recession and new austerity measures may well be introduced. The implications of these changes for minority women are unclear, but we must be wary in terms of how they may erase minority women's experiences and reinforce narratives of the privileged (a theme to which we return in Chapter Six).

In the next chapter, we consider the implications of the French and British austerity regimes in relation to the practices of third sector organisations, and the impact that this has on minority women's activism in each country.

Notes

[1] Admittedly, this issue is difficult to summarise here. As Zakaria Sajir has reminded us (personal correspondence), disaggregation by race and gender is a live issue and a hot topic of debate in France, often covered in the press, and the situation has been evolving with researchers adopting proxies of ethnic/racial categories to get around resistance to ethnic/racial categorisation. Patrick Simon shows in an interesting article (2010:166ff) what sort of alternative strategies researchers employ to circumvent the changing, yet still 'restrictive framework imposed by the French data protection law'. See also Sabbagh and Peer (2008) and the issue of *French Politics, Culture and Society* in which this article appears. Many thanks to Zakaria Sajir for his input here.

[2] According to the definition of the *Haut conseil à l'intégration* ('High Council for Integration') in 1991, and later adopted by the French Institute of Statistics (*Insee*) in subsequent publications, a 'migrant' is a resident who was born a foreigner abroad. This definition of migrant is peculiar to the French case. In fact, in most of the other countries a migrant is an individual who is born abroad. Hence, according to the French definition, an individual who is born abroad and has at least a parent who is French will not be considered as an immigrant. A 'descendant of migrant' is defined as an individual who was born in France from at least a parent who was born abroad. In order to establish the origin of a migrant descendant, the country of birth of the father is considered. Yet if the mother is the only parent who migrated, her country of birth is used instead. Consequently, an 'autochthone' is an individual who did not migrate and who is not a direct descendant of migrants. Although the definition of migrant descendant is not official, this is regularly employed by organisations such as *Insee* (the National Institute of Statistics and Economic Studies) and *Ined* (the National Institute for Demographic Studies).

[3] The 'Minority' group is constituted by 'non-natives, predominantly Africans' (Gobillon et al 2014: 108). The 'Minority' category includes first- and second-generation immigrants from Africa; these sub-categories were identified by virtue of the information on individuals' country of birth, citizenship and first names, gathered for the 1999 French Time Use Survey conducted by the French Institute of Statistics (*Insee*). Importantly, the unemployment figures are calculated on the basis of *Fichier Historique Statistique des Demandeurs d'Emploi* (roughly: Statistical Record of Job Seekers) over the 1996-2003 period, and refer to workers aged 20-65 who resided in the Paris region (Gobillon et al 2014: 110).

[4] ZUS is the acronym used to refer to 'sensitive urban zones'. According to the definition provided by the *Insee*, ZUS are 'infra-urban territories defined by the

authorities as being priority targets for urban policy, according to local factors relating to the difficulties that the inhabitants of these territories are experiencing'. These were created by the law of 14 November 1996 to allow targeted fiscal and social measures in favour of disadvantaged districts. The law identifies 751 ZUS. As shown in a report on the *Observatoire national des zones urbaines sensibles* (L'Horty and Sari 2008), ZUS cannot be perfectly overlapped with the *banlieues*. The ZUS in the Parisian agglomeration represent approximately 23% of the whole ZUS identified; within this agglomeration about 92% of the ZUS are situated in the suburbs. In contrast, in the rest of France, ZUS are situated almost in equal measure within suburbs and town centres (Délégation interministérielle à la ville 2004: 15).

5   Please see: www.runnymedetrust.org/home/scorecard.html

6   The relative poverty level is fixed at 60% of the median of standards of living – that is, 908 euros for 2007.

7   The rule of 'non-remplacement' ('non-replacement') was a measure introduced in 2007 within the framework of the RGPP, *révision générale des politiques publiques* [General Review of Public Policies] and consisted in replacing only one out of every two retiring civil servants (for more details, see Jérôme 2011; Vie Publique 2011; Forum de la performance 2012).

8   The minimum number of months of work necessary before unemployment benefits can be claimed was reduced from six months to four months by virtue of an agreement in December 2008 between a number of French trade unions, such as Confédération française démocratique du travail (CFDT) and the main employers' associations in France, such as MEDEF, UPA, CGPME (for more details, see Libération 2008; Unédic 2009, fiche 1).

9   These were 250 euros for *les bénéficiaires de minima sociaux et d'aide au logement et prime* ('Beneficiaries of Minimum Social Assistance and Housing Assistance') and 150 euros for *les bénéficiaires de l'Allocation de rentrée scolaire* ('Beneficiairies of the Return to School Allocation/Assistance').

10 In France, specifying the 'post-crisis' moment is a matter of debate, with some scholars identifying instead three phases each with their own implications for women: 1. recession; 2. recovery; 3. austerity (Périvier 2014). This tripartite division refers particularly to how the 2008 crisis affected the labour market and the gender gap in different ways, stressing that the worst situation in terms of gender gap started in the austerity phase, when national government started cutting public spending (Marty 2012; Périvier and Silvera 2015).

11 Pension reform more generally has also involved attempts to: progressively close de facto early retirement routes by: abolishing job-search exemptions for older unemployed people; raising minimum and statutory retirement ages; and increasing the effective retirement age by lengthening contribution requirements to claim full pensions (OECD 2012).

FOUR

Enterprising activism

Introduction

In this chapter, we explore how the changing politics of the third sector under austerity problematises minority women's intersectional social justice claims in Scotland, England and France. In particular, we examine how the transformation of the third sector in each country into a 'governable terrain' (Carmel and Harlock 2008) for state social welfare service delivery entrenches an 'enterprise culture' that valorises neoliberal principles and behaviours, which in turn undermines and misrecognises minority women's claims-making.

We define 'enterprise' as encompassing the values of 'individualism, personal achievement … and the assumption of personal responsibility' (Diochon and Anderson 2011: 96). We label the emerging neoliberal practices of the third sector as enterprising, as this seems to capture the twin processes of:

- the privatisation of the state through the contracting out of social welfare services to an array of providers;
- the remodelling of the third sector in the image of the private sector through the inculcation of values and practices related to competition, commodification and individualisation.

Enterprise is often used in the third sector as a synonym for innovation, risk-taking and dynamism. As we demonstrate in this chapter, the market-derived meanings for these terms have been obscured, and these ideas and organisational practices are being promulgated with little thought about what is being invoked (and what is being silenced) in their widespread use. The neoliberal colonisation of the third sector is not a new phenomenon. However, in this moment of economic crisis and instability, what is new, we argue, is the rapidity with which an enterprise culture is being adopted by (and in some cases foisted on) third sector organisations, in order for them to survive in a context of acute resource scarcity.

We begin by exploring the 'governable terrain' of the third sector in Scotland, England and France since the 1990s. It seems that once third sector organisations become the object of state policy – in our cases, as one of the key delivery mechanisms for state social welfare services – this has the (sometimes unintentional) effect of embedding marketised principles and practices, such as individualisation, competition and commodification, in the sector. As the principle of a 'welfare mix' becomes normalised in each country, the reality of having different welfare providers vying for state contracts seems to prompt isomorphic changes, whereby third sector organisations refashion themselves in the image of the private sector as a necessity for survival.

We then move on to discuss the impact that these changes in the third sector are having on minority women's activism. We analyse how the idea of enterprise has become entrenched within these organisations, and how an enterprise culture is problematically reshaping the ways in which organisations think about their mission, practices and programmes of work – especially in relation to minority women.

We conclude with a discussion about what the marketisation of the third sector means for minority women. We argue that political racelessness is enacted through enterprise as minority women's interests are depoliticised and deprioritised through the transformation of the third sector. We suggest that the ability for minority women to articulate and take action on intersectional social justice claims within the sector is under threat, because these claims may well be silenced and/or misrecognised due to the prevailing neoliberal logic of the sector.

Governing the third sector

In Scotland and England

For Scotland and England, it is important to note that third sector governance has been – and continues to be – strikingly similar in both countries. This is despite the more recent Scottish social democratic rhetoric that was linked to the unsuccessful independence referendum in 2014 (Alcock 2012; Emejulu 2015).

John Major's Conservative government policy of contracting out community care services in the early 1990s has proven to be the most influential policy development for the third sector in these two countries. It valourised neoliberal ideas and practices that have become taken for granted today: namely, the development of partnerships between the state and third sector organisations for the 'efficient' delivery of social welfare services (Carmel and Harlock 2008; Milbourne 2013; Emejulu 2015). For the Major government and for the subsequent Labour, Coalition and Conservative governments, developing a governing relationship with the third sector is premised on a marketised logic of privatising the state through the development of a mixed economy of welfare, in which an array of private and third sector providers compete for state contracts to deliver social welfare services. In so doing, it is assumed that the welfare state will become more flexible and efficient in meeting social needs, by driving down costs while simultaneously becoming more democratic and more open to the public.

As third sector organisations grow in importance as key mechanisms for the delivery of state social welfare services, their local and national state partners and their philanthropic funders are slowly refashioning them as objects of policy through governance processes. Carmel and Harlock (2008: 156) persuasively argue that governing the third sector through service delivery partnerships is an ideological act of 'imposing an institutional and normative order' onto a diverse array of voluntary and community organisations that privilege 'market-like behaviour and market-style organisational forms' and 'assumes their necessity'. By the state privileging market-oriented behaviours of third sector organisations, through both resource allocation and sponsorship of particular organisations' policy agendas, these institutional arrangements prompt wider isomorphic transformations of the third sectors in Scotland and England. As Macmillan et al (2013: 3) found in their analysis of third sector organisational behaviour in the context of austerity in England, 'organisations are encouraged [by the state and other philanthropic funders] to become more enterprising, business-like and competitive'. In particular, organisations that would not necessarily conceive of themselves as 'enterprising' are mimicking the behaviours of more 'successful' organisations in terms of their management and leadership structures and the professionalisation of their staff, in order to secure funding and contracts.

We see similar dynamics at play in Scotland. The Commission on the Future Delivery of Public Services, the so-called 'Christie Commission' (2011), was tasked by the Scottish Government to explore state social welfare provision in a context of austerity. Its key message was that: 'Unless Scotland embraces a radical, new, collaborative culture throughout our public services, both budgets and provision will buckle under the strain [of increasing demand and under-funding]'. It recommends 'a fundamental overhaul of the relationships within and between those institutions and agencies – public, third sector and private – responsible for designing and delivering public services'. Exploring the changing nature of Scotland's third sector is under-researched in the literature, and we discuss in more detail in this chapter the isomorphic changes that developments such as the Christie Commission engender in the third sector.

These developments in the third sectors in England and Scotland have been further entrenched and exacerbated by the economic crisis and austerity measures. Third sector organisations in these two countries experience double jeopardy under austerity: as the welfare state is pared back, organisations face increased demand for their services, yet these organisations are operating in a context of acute resource scarcity and fierce competition for dwindling funding (Emejulu and Bassel 2013; Macmillan et al 2013; Bassel and Emejulu 2014).

In response to this dilemma, and as we discuss in more detail later, imitating the successful practices of the private sector and 'enterprising' third sector agencies appears to be the most common strategy that organisations are adopting in order to survive austerity. However, this strategy for organisational survival comes at a cost of limiting 'alternative practices and aspirations' (Milbourne and Cushman 2013: 6) for the third sector, particularly in relation to articulating a new vision for social welfare.

In France

Unlike in Scotland and England, the position of third sector organisations – or *associations*– in France was, until the 1980s, highly ambivalent, because of the republican ethos, shared on both the Left and the Right, that it is the state's role to provide social protection and to ensure *solidarité* through the provision of social welfare services (Chanial and Laville 2004). Importantly, and also unlike in Scotland and England, the process of French associations becoming state social welfare providers *is not necessarily* part of a wider neoliberal project of privatising and marketising the social welfare state, but rather an attempt by state actors to extend the solidarity principle to underserved and overlooked groups (Nicholls 2006; Dikeç 2007; Sintomer and De Maillard 2007).

Since 1968, associations have played a critical role in identifying *la nouvelle pauvreté*: new poverty or 'new' social exclusions generated by changes in the economy, gender relations and migration, which meant that the welfare state was not reaching and supporting particular groups such as the long-term unemployed, survivors of domestic violence and migrants living in neighbourhoods of high deprivation such as *les banlieues*. Associations, locally based and self-organised, provide much-needed social welfare services, while also advocating on behalf of their constituents for the state to respond to those groups experiencing multiple deprivations.[1]

For state actors from the 1980s onwards, by partnering with associations who had expert knowledge of the 'new poor', they could extend the solidarity principle to these groups, while simultaneously reforming the centralised welfare state in order to harness the innovation of associational grassroots practices. For minority and migrant men and women, these developments must also be read in the context of the *mouvement beur*, the antiracist movement of the 1980s that we address in detail in Chapter Five.

Even though the institutionalisation of associations through state partnerships seems to be predicated primarily on the solidarity principle, interestingly, however, the impact of these governance processes appears to have strikingly similar effects as the neoliberal governance of the third sectors in Scotland and England. For example, the state's flagship urban policy, *la politique de la ville*, implemented in one form or another by successive governments from Mitterrand's Socialist government in 1981 to Sarkozy's *Union pour un Mouvement Populaire* government in 2007, placed 'associationalism' at its heart. In an attempt to democratise the centralised welfare state and to extend services to groups whom the welfare state had previously failed to reach, state actors 'were required to develop a bureaucratic infrastructure to coordinate broad and complex partnerships [with associations] and ensure a degree of uniformity across project sites' (Nicholls 2006: 1780). By transforming previously independent grassroots organisations into policy objects, this seems to have had the effect of 'compell[ing] individual associations to professionalise, politicise and individualise their actions'. Consequently, the 'associational sectors of many deprived neighbourhoods have ceased being a medium of articulating grievances of residents and expressing grievances to the state' (Nicholls 2006: 1780).

Thus, there seems to be something about the ways in which welfare states – at least those in Scotland, England and France – institutionalise third sector organisations that prompt isomorphic transformations and encourage the abandonment of alternative and oppositional practices of these organisations. It is important to note that the French state has not escaped neoliberal restructuring, but that neoliberalism, as a process, has been adapted to the particular institutional arrangements of republicanism. It is in the context of the ongoing economic crisis and austerity that, we argue, the latent neoliberal processes under way in France are brought sharply into focus.

We explore the particular ways in which neoliberalism is expressed in the French third sector – and the implications of this in relation to minority women's activism – in our discussion of our findings later in this chapter. We will now explore the enterprising organisational practices of the third sectors in Scotland, England and France, and examine the impact on minority women's activism.

The enterprising third sector and minority women's activism

Our findings demonstrate that the impact of austerity on third sector organisations in Scotland, England and France was experienced in similar ways, through:

- budget cuts;
- staff redundancies;
- the closure of organisations;
- mergers of different organisations;
- reductions in staff working hours;
- cuts to service provision.

In our interviews with third sector workers, however, what we found most striking was the development and expansion of ideas and organisational practices linked to enterprise as both a survival strategy and an imposed solution on organisations by the local and national state and large philanthropic funders. We found that the rise of an enterprise culture impacts on third sector organisations in two interrelated ways: it marketises the relationships *between organisations*; and imposes privatised norms and values *within organisations*. These changes to the third sector, we argue, have disastrous consequences for minority women's activism.

Marketising third sector relations

Due to the unprecedented budget cuts of the French and British austerity programmes, this seems to have transformed once 'friendly rivals' into fierce competitors for a shrinking pool of funding. The changing funding environment has meant that cooperation and mutuality within the sector are being displaced by competition and bidding wars between different third sector organisations, and between the third sector and private sector organisations, to secure state social welfare service contracts.

In a typical illustration of this phenomenon in Lyon, a caseworker at a migrants' rights centre described the following scenario in which: "Solidarity between associations doesn't exist". He described a particular organisation that was in a political conflict with the Prefect of the region. The association had done its work well, but it was suddenly subject to frequent audits and finally had its state contract unfairly cancelled. Rather than protesting the arbitrary decision to cancel this organisation's contract, 'associational colleagues' instead hurried to submit rival bids to secure this newly available service delivery contract (Participant FR1).

A director of an anti-poverty organisation in Edinburgh identified a similar process at work:

> 'From my own experience of working in the voluntary sector for a long time, is you could work with other agencies around and agree not to fight over the funding and have a united stance to say we want this [funding] split up fairly but now I think there's more cut-throat competition for funding.' (Participant SC1)

This phrase 'cut-throat competition' is repeated across several of our interviews in terms of participants' describing the changing nature of relationships within the sector. As we discuss later, this seems to indicate that solidarity within the sector is degrading.

We see similar issues at play in England, as a director of a migrants' rights organisation in London (see Appendix) observed:

> 'There is less money [available] you know and so I think people who are competing to run public services, now there are a lot of sharks around and there is a lot of fear of their capacity, a huge capacity of the big organisations to basically marketise the work that we have done as a community.' (Participant EN1)

The logic of cut-throat competition has also ushered in other enterprising strategies and tactics: mergers, acquisitions and organisations' vying for new market share of particular social problems. This strategy – of organisations treating social problems as a 'market' to enter, compete in and to exploit for their future survival – surprised us by how deeply and uncritically neoliberal practices had penetrated the sector. For example, some of our participants noted that as grant-in-aid funding had been cut, this had engendered fierce competition for state contracts. However, even though enterprising work was mandated by the state and by many philanthropic funders, this was not a realistic model for all third sector organisations, putting their survival at risk. As one director of a public health organisation in Glasgow noted:

'I think what many of the projects are having to do is move from grant aid thinking … into social enterprise thinking and income generating thinking and that's fine up to a point if you've got something to trade but if you're working with people who are drug users or [with] people with mental health problems, you don't have a lot to trade.' (Participant SC2)

Smaller, specialist organisations, particularly those led by minority women, are, as a consequence, disappearing or being swallowed up by larger organisations as a way for those large organisations to burnish their credentials in relation to a particular social problem in order capture new market share in bidding for available state contracts. A development worker in a statutory organisation in London observed that the third sector is slowly being reshaped by the dominance of large organisations competing for state social welfare contracts:

'The small organisations are suffering because all these bids and things are only possible if … you have a very big organisation behind you, so the third sector is really the "big third sector" not the "small third sector". I think the small third sector is sort of disappearing because the grassroots worker is not there anymore.' (Participant EN2)

Several participants in London observed the disappearance of smaller third sector organisations that are serving minority communities, a concern that is expressed more broadly in the 'Black and minority ethnic sector' following the economic downturn (see also ROTA 2009; CEMVO 2010; and on challenging the claim that BME organisations fare worse, Mayblin and Soteri-Proctor 2011).

A development worker for a minority women-led organisation in Edinburgh observed a similar phenomenon north of the border:

'I think we've become very competitive with each other … because there is this move within local authorities to tender the services that they now give us grant funding for. And what that means is that if you [a large mainstream organisation] say "we will work with black minority ethnic women as well" … then you're more likely to get the funding … In their desire to survive and to convince the funders that they are inclusive of everyone, we are losing the need for specialist organisations, and specialist organisations have to fight harder to justify their existence.' (Participant SC3)

Perhaps unsurprisingly in this context of increased competition and jockeying for market share on particular social problems, there was a perception among several participants that state service delivery contracts were undermining alternative forms of collective action within the third sector, especially building solidarity across organisations to undertake oppositional work against particular policy priorities of local and national governments. In other words, the third sectors in Scotland, England and France were experiencing a 'chilling effect', self-censorship in order to retain their state contracts. For example, a caseworker at a militant migrants' rights association in Paris observed:

'There are associations financed 100% by the state … for whom the margin for manoeuvre is very limited. They are limited politically for a very simple reason … [By] not responding to bidding calls and calls for tender … or imposing conditions and limits on the Office of Immigration and Integration by saying, "We won't go into that field, we won't work for less than that, we will not receive immigrants under these minimal conditions" … is taking a risk at a time where associations financed by the state are being put in competition with one another.' (Participant FR2)

A policy manager at an anti-poverty organisation in Glasgow echoed a similar sentiment:

'Increasingly organisations that have got funding relationships with government agencies are feeling that they can't speak out … Organisations are feeling that they need to be silent because of those funding relationships [with the state] that they need to protect.' (Participant SC4)

The caseworker at the militant migrants' rights association in Paris put the issue of third sector oppositional work in blunt terms:

'The reality is that the state more or less say[s] "We're the ones who finance you. The stakes are these … we remind you there'll be calls for tender" and if we don't respond [to these terms] someone else will.' (Participant FR2)

Of course, we do not wish to suggest that the pre-austerity relationships within the third sector in each country were unproblematic. Indeed, there is a longstanding critique of third sector organisations being easily co-opted and constrained by both state and private sector actors through funding relationships and of third sector organisations undermining radical analyses and actions of social movements (Kamat 2004; Choudry and Shragge 2011; Choudry and Kapoor 2013). What we argue is that austerity has further legitimised an enterprise culture that appears to erode solidaristic work between third sector organisations, and it also appears to create a chilling effect that prevents some organisations from undertaking oppositional work against the state and private sector actors. We now turn to explore how a marketised logic has penetrated the culture within organisations.

Marketising organisational norms and values

In our interviews, we found that an enterprise culture also appeared to undermine organisations' norms, values and goals. Many of the organisations we interviewed were being restructured due to budget cuts and having to do more work with fewer staff and resources. The moment of restructuring seemed to create the conditions for the embedding of a marketised logic within the organisation. A third sector worker in Paris put it in these terms:

'There is a desire [from the state] to express social work in terms of a service which we do not agree with, meaning that the people we support are not consumers of a service … When we support someone we don't just respond to their demands, we support them in formulating demands. So it is something different and we try to support [people] with tools of social work and not tools of marketing. So for us it is very different to speak in terms of social work and to speak in terms of service provision.' (Participant FR3)

In particular, the staff's intense focus on the operational and fundraising aspects of organisational survival – especially in the bidding for contracts and/or transforming themselves into social enterprises – appeared to be preventing some of them from thinking critically and strategically about their mission, purpose and practices, especially in a context of austerity. A caseworker at a migrants' rights organisation in Paris observed:

> 'Most of my colleagues … have their nose to the grindstone from morning to night and they don't necessarily realise what's happening on the ground or what's at stake. Indeed, sometimes the way in which the situation is represented makes them say "*Oh là là*, the sword of Damocles … will we be able to keep our jobs or not?"' (Participant FR2)[2]

This overwork and under-analysis of the toll that the new funding regime was having on third sector workers' critical capacities was also noted by the director of an anti-poverty organisation in Edinburgh:

> '[These new funding arrangements] take away from the staff teams … to be able to think and develop new ways of working because you're actually doing very intense work and [the] headspace quite often then isn't there to be able to think, "How do we develop this service?"' (Participant SC1)

A migrants' rights development manager in London identified a lack of time and resources as a key challenge to joining efforts, rather than working separately:

> 'I suppose we don't really have that many opportunities to have those kinds of [critical] conversations [with colleagues] … You know a lot of this working together business is a luxury, actually. You need to have time to put in and you know, at the moment, my free time is from midnight to five a.m.!' (Participant EN3)

The issue of overwork and the conflict this causes with home life was a key theme running through many of our interviews. Our only Wales-based participant articulated the unsustainable balancing act she must perform between the pressures at work and at home, which left little time for critical reflection:

> 'I have a very young family. And that [third sector] organisation is taking too much of my time … Yeah despite our passion, despite our goodwill, we can't keep on doing

it. I will not keep on doing it ... I have a young family.'
(Participant WA1)

For third sector organisations, doing more with less in a context of austerity seems to prevent some workers from thinking critically and strategically about the implications of their work with their constituent groups. Austerity also means that an enterprise logic is also seeping into some organisations' ethos and behaviour. As the director of the anti-poverty organisation in Edinburgh argues:

'I think that's a critical weakness in the way things are developing ... [The enterprise culture] doesn't acknowledge the fact that as third sector organisations you're more than just the arm of the local state, you're not just there to deliver their services for them, it's a different ethos and you do have your own organisational ethos and priorities as well which are supporting local authority and national government priorities and outcomes but third sector organisations shouldn't be shoehorned into doing it in one way only.'
(Interview SC1)

A social worker at a housing association for women in Paris agrees:

'It's our identity as an association [that's at stake]. If it's to become a business in the plans and work methods, isn't it better for a business to take the job over? Or that one admits one is no longer an association? But for us ... an organisation that has always been a force of critique, it's very complicated for us to position ourselves [in the new enterprise environment].' (Participant FR4)

For this director of a migrants' rights organisation in London, the pressure to innovate displaced his work of service delivery:

'What I think the problem for our sector is we haven't got the capacity to scale. So we have got the capacity to innovate, we haven't got the capacity to scale. So to some extent you are always having to sort of reinvent your innovation, you have always got to be the innovative agency, you can't be the mass deliverer.' (Participant EN1)

As we have demonstrated, austerity represents both a material and an ideological crisis for third sector organisations. Not only do they have to negotiate unprecedented budget cuts, but they must also attend to the marketised values that austerity advances. Many of our participant organisations were caught in a bind of trying to ensure the survival of their organisation, while maintaining their political, professional and organisational values. We will now turn to exploring the impact of these changes in the third sector on minority women's activism.

Minority women activists: entrepreneurs, victims or invisible?

Activists as entrepreneurs in Scotland and England

In Scotland and England, for those organisations that actively embrace an enterprise culture, many appeared to be motivated by a search for new ways of empowering disadvantaged groups, and it was assumed that an enterprise model provides a dynamism not previously present in the sector. By adopting an enterprising approach, third sector organisations would be in a stronger position to deliver effective services for their constituents, because they would be in a more powerful position in relation to the state. As a director of a community development organisation in Edinburgh argues:

> 'I don't think that communities can take control without controlling assets and controlling services ... or some business. I think you need to have some substance to become a player and I don't think you can do that without having some sort of enterprising approach.' (Participant SC5)

In Scotland in particular, we found that minority women activists are being recast by some third sector organisations as 'enterprising actors', meaning that activists' critical analyses of their intersectional inequalities are being reshaped and channelled into neoliberal work: specifically, the instituting of social enterprises such as community cafes, crèches and sewing groups. The embedding of an enterprise culture among activists was justified by a policy manager of an anti-poverty organisation in Glasgow using the language of empowerment whereby:

> 'A more of a level playing field [with the state is created].
> It's somebody commissioning a service and it's somebody

providing a service ... The balance of power in that is always really interesting ... They're [minority women] more business partners than they are donor and recipient and that is an angle we would definitely like to try.' (Participant SC4)

Several activist minority women we interviewed in Glasgow and Edinburgh expressed deep scepticism of this approach, because they were unconvinced that micro-level enterprising work could have a meaningful impact on the intersecting inequalities they experience, such as discrimination within the asylum system, everyday experiences of racism in their neighbourhoods and labour market discrimination. Here we can see how political racelessness is enacted through enterprise to depoliticise minority women's activism and deprioritise their interests.

As a West African migrant activist in Glasgow noted:

'The problems that minority ethnic women face are more structured in nature and therefore beyond the power of the community themselves to actually change.' (Participant SC6)

A development worker for an anti-poverty organisation in Glasgow, who works with the activist just mentioned (Participant SC6), was pushing ahead with an enterprising approach for the migrant women with whom she works, despite the reservations articulated by the activists:

'We're shifting towards more enterprise oriented activities rather than just grants ... Grant funding isn't the way the future's going and self-generation of funding is important ... It's helped communities experiencing poverty set up their own enterprises and to get a toe-hold in the market system.' (Participant SC7)

The issue here is about the disconnect between minority women's experiences and analyses of their precarity (which we will discuss more in Chapter Five) and the type of projects and programmes offered by third sector organisations undergoing the isomorphic transformations into quasi-private sector organisations we discussed earlier in this chapter. Particularly in Scotland, we found that minority women activists were not being listened to and their views about the meaning and purpose of their activism was misrecognised by many of their third sector partners.

Further complicating matters for minority women's activism in Scotland, was the widespread perception among our activist participants that their neighbourhoods are hostile territories that undermine their activism and attempts to build solidarity among different local groups. In one focus group with activist migrant women in Glasgow, participants were very doubtful that they could form effective links with white Scots to talk about their shared experiences of poverty and economic inequality, because of the everyday racism they experienced in their neighbourhoods. As one West African activist argued:

> 'Ethnic minority groups [are] trying to drive in their humble way different causes, but how do you link with the local people, the indigenous people? It's almost impossible … You don't seem to find an avenue to join in when people are doing their thing, so you somehow find yourself on the sidelines all the time. Even if you did your thing, you won't be able to attract them [white Scots] to come with you [because] it's so segregated.' (Participant SC8)

Another West African focus group participant concurred:

> 'I could kind of see that the fact that, you know, people are in crisis could also mean that they will be more hateful towards migrants. Migrants are quite easy targets because … they [white Scots] don't feel they [migrants] belong to this country … So it's very easy to target migrants and I'm one of them.' (Participant SC9)

Because these activist women do not experience a real sense of 'community' in their neighbourhoods because of the racism, hostility and isolation they experience, this appears to stop them (and of course their white neighbours as well) from forming grassroots coalitions based on shared grievances. These findings point to another obstacle to minority women's activism in Scotland. As third sector organisations are increasingly constituted by enterprising work and as communities are perceived as hostile spaces, there appears to be little opportunity to build shared meanings and experiences of inequality, making coalition-building extremely challenging for minority women. Here we see the paradox of political racelessness in action. Race, assumed to be a settled matter in Scotland, is set aside, while the racial contract of white supremacy is enforced in everyday social relations.

In England, particularly in London, participants identified similar neighbourhood divisions, based on race and legal status, that have been exacerbated by particular anti-immigrant government initiatives such as the Home Office's notorious 'Go Home or Face Arrest' van campaigns. Some of our participants also reported how divisive policies were, such as a London borough providing funding to community organisations, including women's groups, to persuade homeless migrants involved in sex work to return to their country of origin (Knowledge Exchange Event, London, February 2014). Clearly, this is a harsher discursive and policy context than in Scotland. However, as we observed, this xenophobic climate also galvanises opposition in distinct ways, for example opposition to the 'Go Home' vans that resulted in the campaign being abandoned by the government.

This refugee activist in London echoed the challenge of hostility to migrants at the neighbourhood level. She recounted the reactionary views of a 'British' woman she was supporting in the course of her work in providing information to parents about changes in welfare reform:

> '[There is] this mother who was also British, born British, raised British, had three children, she worked for 17 years in this country then she had an illness that stopped her working. Now she's been affected by the benefit cap ... but she's not saying, "okay, we are in recession, there is crisis, we have to pay this and the Government has made these changes", but she's saying, "I am born and raised British, why should I be affected by something that foreigners caused?" So somehow the blame for all these changes that are happening at the moment is pointed towards migrants and that will increase racism, discrimination, specifically against migrant families.' (Participant EN4)

However, we found a different process at play regarding the space that is created for minority women's activism by enterprising third sector organisations. It seems that some minority women are able to use social enterprises as a tool for advocacy and activism. An activist refugee woman chose to establish a social enterprise because she perceived it to be a less bureaucratic and more responsive space for intervention. Directing a social enterprise, she argues:

> 'Gives me the independence that I need. We need to earn our money through the expertise we deliver ... and [we] then [get] to decide [how] to spend the money on

the services that we feel are needed. So it gives me that independence, not only that, although I have an advisory role I make the decisions so it gives [organisation's name] power to decide on its own.' (Participant EN4)

This participant uses 'information sessions' organised by her social enterprise as an opportunity to move beyond explaining to people how they will be affected by the government's welfare reform programme to raising awareness (particularly of single female-headed migrant households) of their rights to contest decisions, notably when eviction looms as a result of loss of housing benefits and/or employment. This is particularly important in the context of cuts to legal aid (Sommerlad and Sanderson 2013). As she explains:

> 'It's very important to inform people, for them to understand what their rights are, and whether they can join campaigns or whether they can do something.' (Participant EN4)

This activist's important work points to the possibility of subverting the ideology of an enterprise culture by using 'enterprise' as a cover for supporting minority women's social citizenship rights and anti-austerity activism. This social entrepreneur is enacting her activism through an enterprising approach and this has undoubtedly opened up opportunities to address the asymmetrical impact of cuts on minority women and displace the political racelessness in enterprising work.

In Manchester, a British Indian social entrepreneur found freedom in an enterprise model. She argues that social enterprises are an important form of activism and it is through her social enterprise that she experiences a sense of belonging and agency:

> 'We are a very unique organisation in terms of creating a culture of expressive freedom ... and don't really see ourselves bound by the shackles of public funding or partnerships. I think it's [social enterprise] a very important and effective tool in achieving change, activism, justice, increased economic growth ... You'll find that people who work in social enterprises have ... a greater sense of belonging and feel they have the power to make change.' (Participant EN5)

However, as our Scottish data suggest, as discussed earlier, taking an enterprising approach does not necessarily always match minority women's interests and priorities – and may, in fact, reinforce political racelessness and the racial contract. We question the extent to which enterprising third sector organisations are open to being shaped by minority women and their interests rather than an enterprise logic dictating the terms of minority women's activism. Indeed, a more typical response to social enterprise in England was one of pragmatism for organisational survival, as seen in this response from a development worker in Coventry:

> 'I would question whether, at the end of the day, their [third sector workers] interest is in what's the benefit of their service users or is it in the interest of the people in their organization … I'm the same. I had this idea for the cooking and the cleaning [service] but I never spoke to any women [with whom she works] about it. I just thought what skills have the women got, where they haven't got high literacy or numeracy levels. They haven't got high levels of qualifications. But they can bloody cook.' (Participant EN6)

Our two participants who found relative freedom rather than constraint in an enterprise culture in England (Participant EN4 and Participant EN5)) were unique among the activists we interviewed. That spaces are available for subversion of the enterprise logic is important to highlight and demonstrates that enterprise can be used for subversion. Nevertheless, the important, more general point is the extent to which 'enterprise' appears to be a demand that activists working with and through the third sectors in Scotland and England cannot seem to refuse or avoid – and how enterprise reinforces political racelessness. The ways in which minority women can and do position themselves around an enterprising culture, and their ability to resist the neoliberal logic of enterprise, requires further scrutiny and comparison.

On being invisible or instrumentalised in France

In France, the challenges for migrant women's activism and advocacy in third sector organisations predate the 2008 economic crisis and must be situated in an associational landscape that was already characterised by *either* women's organisations *or* migrant organisations (Bassel 2012). As a caseworker at a migrants' rights centre in Paris observes: 'There are few associations that do both: women and foreigners [*étrangers*]' (Participant FR5).

Reduced service provision and limited sources of funding make it difficult, but not impossible, to mobilise around minority women's intersectional justice claims. This is either because of the intention to work with undocumented women, who are excluded from some forms of European funding, or because their work is on a local rather than national scale, which excludes them from French funding streams that aim to include migrant women. In France, we see political racelessness enacted as official policy of the Republic. The difficulty of moving across categories of difference in order to undertake activism and advocacy that speaks to race, class, gender and legal status simultaneously appears to render minority women activists invisible in some of the French third sector spaces in our study.

The lack of intersectional work on race, class, gender and legal status was justified by some third sector workers in our study on republican grounds: they expressed this as a need to avoid 'ghettoes' whereby 'specialist' services would lead to segregation, placing some women outside of '*le droit commun*' [common law/shared rights]. One male housing worker in Paris objected to 'women-only' housing services, which leads to:

> 'leaving violent men alone … and as a result we are no longer in *le droit commun*. We are hyperspecialising any given problem which is in the hands of specialists and not the problem of a society to resolve itself.' (Participant FR6)

In other words, specialist services, in themselves, undermine social solidarity by removing social problems from the public sphere for all citizens to work to resolve.

A similar claim was made by a white French woman activist regarding specialist services for sex workers:

> 'This is why I take the precaution of saying that at a moment in their [sex workers'] trajectory, it's necessary to have specialised support. But the goal of our work is to lead to something generalist, toward *le droit commun* [common/shared law]. So for example, we need a stage of specialised shelters but after when looking for suitable housing we have … [housing facilities] … that are open to everyone because we don't want to make a ghetto of people who have known prostitution [sic]. So there is a danger of the ghetto but this depends at what stage they [sex workers] are.' (Participant FR3)

This fear of the 'ghetto' is a longstanding spectre in France. It haunts the universal, indivisible and difference-blind Republic, and is seamlessly reproduced by third sector actors, including those in migrant advocacy organisations who have been resistant to recognition of gender-based persecution experienced by refugee women for similar reasons (Freedman 2007; Bassel 2012).

For those activists and advocates in our study who do seek to respond to the problem of crossing categories of difference to make intersectional claims, they use the frame of 'victimhood' in order to advance minority women's interests. As a jurist who advocates on behalf of minority women described it, the 'victim' angle 'works' and is difficult to refuse:

> 'One thing that's certain is that the prism of foreign women [as] victims of violence [is very effective]. We're able to have more of an impact with politicians because no one supports violence. So it's an angle of attack that's interesting [and] useful.' (Participant FR5)

This advocate has been able to successfully lobby civil servants, party officials and elected members in both the current *Parti Socialiste* and the former *Union pour un Mouvement Populaire* governments to speak about minority women's precarity and domestic violence. Victimhood, therefore, provides an opportunity for some participants in our study to make minority women visible and to mobilise support for them across the political spectrum.

A minority woman activist made a similar claim about the resonance of victimhood across the political spectrum, noting that helping women who are victims of violence was supposedly as much a priority for the current President Hollande as for the former President Sarkozy. However, in her experience she was consulted and listened to much more by right-wing governments than those on the Left (which was where her own political sympathies lie). She described being invited by a UMP government minister to speak for two hours about how she thought new migrants should be received and, specifically, what measures should be taken for migrant women:

> 'Two hours, two hours I said my blah, blah, the two councillors took notes. After two hours he [the minister] said to me "Of course I can't say that everything you've said suits me, or will suit me, but I thank you very much. You've given me a lot of ideas that I will take into account." I said

to myself "*Merde*, this is incredible." Why? Because after I thought about it and I checked after because I think the French Right, who is always accused of not being "social" enough, needs to consult widely and doesn't have a problem with this. You can be a militant communist and they will ask you face-to-face what you think about a certain technical subject. They consult. Afterwards they do what they want, but they consult. Whereas the Left thinks that among their ranks, in the ranks of the party, there are people who know things and they only consult people who are ideologically close to them. But that is completely false because just because someone doesn't share your ideology doesn't mean they are incompetent.' (Participant FR7)

The problem here, in the difference-blind Republic, lies beyond these party cleavages, in the fact that minority women's possibility for visibility and audibility lies primarily in a perceived victimhood and victim identity. The associational and political landscape is unable to recognise the intersectional inequalities and agency of minority women. Activists are rendered invisible because of the particular structure of state funding, or they must adopt an identity as a 'victim' in order to be (mis)recognised in policy debates. Thus minority women in France have a distinct and ongoing problem, which is different (but related) to their counterparts in England and Scotland: as austerity is reshaping the organisational ethos and practices of the third sector, minority women activists must also advocate for basic recognition in these increasingly neoliberal spaces.

However, a caseworker at a militant migrants' rights organisation in Paris found that despite the organisational changes that austerity has wrought, this was a moment of opportunity for radical action with and for migrant women, because austerity has:

'A positive effect on militant action … This [action] isn't achieved by those financed by the state … People, refugees, asylum seekers, will turn more toward solidarity in the receiving country, basic solidarity … [Under conditions of] austerity, it's more or less positive because it will reinforce this militant side that isn't connected to the state and that's more independent.' (Participant FR8)

This kind of independence was also fiercely maintained by housing rights activists, who mobilise using a model of collective organisation, as a kind of trade union for the *mal logés* [the poorly housed] funded by membership fees and donations. They explicitly state that they have no ambition to run shelters or to find housing, but instead to fight for people's rights to be protected. As one of the activists described it:

> 'This means that sometimes people come to see us … and sure, it is to have an apartment for a certain time. In all cases you have to really be with us to increase our presence, our visibility, so we can be effective and so we get results, and then, at that moment, we distribute equally according to the results we've achieved.' (Participant FR9)

However, we are concerned about the extent to which these 'independent' movements, particularly against austerity, recognise minority women as legitimate political actors and make space for their activism. How do these movements reproduce or undermine political racelessness? On whose terms are these mobilisations structured, which claims are articulated and who speaks on whose behalf? Our research took place 2011 to 2014, and since the conclusion of our study, we have seen the emergence of the *Nuit Debout* movement[3] in response to the new *loi travail* [labour law], which seems to erode security and protection in work. Early analysis of *Nuit Debout* appears to show that these protest spaces are dominated by white male voices and bodies, and exclude minority women's analyses and interests (Wdowiak 2016).

As an enterprise culture is further entrenched in the third sectors in Scotland, England and France, the sectors, in turn, transmit these neoliberal ideas and practices to their constituent groups. As the third sector increasingly resembles the private sector, the groups with whom it works must be recast as clients, entrepreneurs or victims but not necessarily as *citizens* with particular political, social and economic rights. For minority women activists, this process of being represented as an 'enterprising actor' in Scotland and England, or by being rendered invisible or misrecognised as a 'victim' in France, undermines the ability for women to organise and mobilise on the inequalities they experience, particularly in relation to austerity. Many minority women become instrumentalised in reproducing political racelessness. Transforming minority women activists into entrepreneurs or victims is an attempt to deny their agency and their analysis – this is the operation of the racial contract. There are opportunities outside the formal third sector for minority women to be recognised as active agents and citizens, and we will discuss this in more detail in Chapter Five.

Conclusions

In this chapter, we have attempted to explore what happens to third sector organisations when they become objects of state policy through governance arrangements and the impact this has on minority women's activism. In ostensibly opposite contexts of 'multicultural' Scotland and England and 'republican' France, we find similar issues at play: when third sector organisations enter into partnership arrangements with the state to deliver social welfare services, this appears to prompt isomorphic transformations of the wider sector. This entrenches an enterprising culture of competition and marketisation that displaces oppositional action against particular policy priorities.

The knock-on effect of the third sector's isomorphic transformation is that minority women's activism in third sector spaces appears to be undermined. We suggest that in the current crisis, the third sector experiences austerity not only as acute resource scarcity but also as ideological domination. Budget cuts, staff redundancies and organisational restructurings represent a material and ideological crisis for many organisations, and an enterprise culture is presented by both the state and by philanthropic funders as the only path to organisational survival. In a context of third sector organisations' cut-throat relationships with each other – and where practitioners are disciplined into neoliberal ways of working – there appear to be rapidly shrinking spaces in which minority women activists articulate and advance their intersectional social justice claims.

We will now explore the fate of activists working outside these third sector spaces.

Notes

[1] The French third sector is composed of three types of organisations: cooperatives, mutuals and associations. Cooperatives and mutuals are quasi-market organisations, while associations are distinguished by traditionally providing social services for those groups poorly served by the centralised welfare state: the long-term unemployed, undocumented migrants, women with experiences of domestic violence, and so on (Chanial and Laville 2004). We included only associations in our study.

[2] In turn, new developments in hiring, requiring 'professional' social work staff with certified training and state diplomas, were also perceived as a way of suppressing militancy within service provision organisations.

[3] *Nuit Debout* is a populist movement sparked by the introduction of the Socialist government's new *loi travail* [labour law] that attempts to liberalise the French labour market by weakening worker protections. Inspired by Occupy and *Los Indignados*, *Nuit Debout* protestors camp in public squares and engage in radical education on economic inequality.

FIVE

The politics of survival

Introduction

In this chapter, we explore minority women's strategies for survival in informal spaces: self-help groups, DIY networks and grassroots community organisations, as well as our participants' personal narratives of, and reflections on, coping within neoliberal third sector organisations. As we discussed in Chapter One, we seek to redefine 'what counts' and who enjoys the identity of 'activist', by naming and analysing minority women's politics of survival. Recognising and valuing the political actions of minority women in both public and private spaces is central to our understandings of minority women's political behaviour in Europe. Throughout this book, we have defined 'activism' broadly in order to capture the diverse ways in which minority women assert themselves as political agents. Here we turn our focus to the grassroots and personal narratives.

We argue that minority women's activism is either misrecognised or erased by the white Left because, as we discussed in Chapter Two, socialist, populist and feminist theories and politics, imbued with political racelessness, are hostile to discussions of race, ethnicity and migration as they fracture 'universal' understandings of the 'working class' and 'women'. Given this hostility to intersectional politics, this problematises minority women's politics of self-care and the solidarity work that minority women activists seek to build with their white counterparts.

We centre the activism of minority women and note that it is often connected to third sector spaces and should not be dismissed as 'inauthentic' for this reason. Yet we also demonstrate that no space is immune from 'enterprise' (explored in the previous chapter), and show the ways in which context matters in each case to limit as well as frame minority women's activism as a politics of survival. In Chapter Four, we saw the ways in which particular features of the French, Scottish and English cases shape what is possible for, with and by minority women in the formal third sector. Here we see what is being done and what can be done in these informal spaces. These spaces are sometimes depleted by austerity, sexism and racism but are also sites of resistance.

We conclude by demanding that this politics of survival be recognised as a first step towards solidarity and alliances.

Personal and collective resources

In material terms, the economic crisis has taken a toll on everyday life and the personal and collective resources for minority women's activism. Some minority women are particularly disadvantaged due to precarious employment, legal status and/or greater reliance on dwindling public services, as we explored in Chapter Three. The seemingly prosaic and routine hardships that some women experience have profound impacts on their activism – for instance, a lack of affordable childcare; diminished core funding for minority women-led organisations; the withdrawal of funding for transport costs to attend meetings in rooms that are no longer provided free of charge.

We argue that minority women need to navigate *both* material *and* discursive obstacles – about whose crisis counts, who is a legitimate interlocutor, and who can mobilise for social justice. As Janet Newman argues, it is increasingly difficult for women activists to find time or resources for 'creative political work' because 'cuts in public and welfare services are intensifying the time pressures … making it more difficult to reconcile care work, paid employment, casual work, study, voluntary or charitable contributions and political activity' (Newman 2013: 217; see also Lonergan 2015). For example, a Scottish Pakistani woman volunteering at a minority women-led community organisation in Glasgow stated:

> 'We've got a lot of stuff we have to do. Like the kids' breakfast and stuff, it's mainly us women that are doing it. Bringing and dropping them off at schools, even at the mosque, that's mainly women that's doing that. So it [cuts to services] does [have an impact], it quite tires a woman out. When it comes to the weekend when you want to spend time with the kids more, you're more reluctant, [you want] to be staying in bed.' (CRER Participant 2)

Our only Wales-based participant, whose experiences we explored in Chapter Four, articulated a theme common across all cases: the direct competition between activism and family caring responsibilities (see also Bassel and Emejulu, forthcoming 2018). She identifies a zero-sum relationship between family life and her third sector activism, time she cannot spend with her kids, sleeping, studying (Participant WA1).

For a Black activist in London, the cuts are indeed having a detrimental effect on minority women's activism:

> 'If you've got a family, you're a single parent, you're a Black woman who is probably working two jobs [with] unsociable shifts, you've got tyrant-type bosses who if you're one minute late they're ready to sack you and you're not in secure employment where they can just sack you and get you of the door and get somebody in the next day, then you really haven't got time and you're probably too tired to get up and start campaigning around things.' (Participant EN7)

In France, some minority women activists described 'great discouragement' that was being transmitted across generations. In one case, an older woman was mentoring a younger activist who was trying to continue to provide minority woman-led support to women of her own background and who had experienced different forms of violence. The older woman describes the younger as saying:

> 'I'm fed up [j'en ai marre], I'm fed up of fighting, to not have Saturdays, to not have Sundays, to not have evenings and on top of this to work on never ending files for hours and hours for peanuts and all these hours I take them away from women who need me.' (Participant FR7)

The older woman goes on to comment:

> 'And she is young, a young woman ... if at [her age] she is discouraged, I've led an association for 25 years and also started with peanuts, but this means that something is not right because if so little hope is given to *militants* [activists] who give their time and energy for low salaries to do this public work, well you can't expect that they will do it all their lives because it is always at the expense of something else, and I think it is the same depression at [names two other minority women-led organisations].' (Participant FR7)

These minority women activists have created local, grassroots initiatives that receive little or no money, are not being listened to, and too often disappear because, as Participant FR7 terms it, there is a 'demobilisation of energies'.

When interviewed, the younger minority woman activist described insecurity and relentless emotional labour, trying to work with women from other cultural backgrounds to her own (where she cannot deploy the same specialist knowledge and understanding), the attempts to fund her work and to support women effectively:

> 'It is not just to listen because there has to be real support until this person is autonomous and that is my way of doing things, it is my conviction ... I do not play with people's lives ... To work with a woman is to take responsibility for her life in my hands. This means to help her get by ... and I will fight for her. So I succeed with her or I lose with her, but her loss is my loss ... I cannot see their destruction because it is unbearable for me, when I work it is with my guts, unfortunately or fortunately, I don't know.' (Participant FR10)

Generally, she is 'psychologically tired':

> 'I tell myself "Do something else with your life, turn to other things, try to forget this whole social sphere where you have been" ... because it is super tiring, it is very heavy to carry psychologically.' (Participant FR10)

This fatigue – both mental and political – has also adversely affected volunteering as a vehicle for activism in Scotland, England and France. One French observer noted that associations are in a logic of defence rather than attack due to austerity measures, and because of this, *militantes* [female activists] many of whom in their case are volunteers, are 'more and more tired' because of exploitative volunteer work ['*un phenomène d'usure*'] (Participant FR11).

In one case, volunteering seemed to undermine political work. Volunteering was identified as a means of survival, as an employment strategy, but not as a political practice for minority women in small migrant communities in Edinburgh to advance their interests:

> 'We are here to earn money and to make lives for ourselves, activism is not really for a minority community and I think that's a sort of a prevalent environment in Edinburgh because we are quite small. I think in London you will find differences or maybe in Glasgow because it's much bigger so there's greater chance to find an activist. I don't

think, personally I don't think that anybody who works in [organisation] would do it for free, they do it because they get a job … even if you have migrated a generation or may be two generations you know you're still putting your roots into the ground, still the memory of possible poverty when you arrived is still alive, the responsibilities of sending money back home are still alive. So most of your decisions are based around money and volunteering, it's not even an option for many or it's not something you do… We are still trying to fit in and we are still seeing, the world still sees us as people who only came here to be economically active, the rest of the world, so we still have that cultural mindset and new migrants certainly, we are not here to change the world. If we wanted to change the world we would have stayed where we were … Some of it is my own view but I think even from the women we see, very few of them will take active steps to make things better collectively.' (Participant SC11)

As we can see, economic insecurity creates real dilemmas for minority women's activism, even in this last case pitting 'politics' against 'survival'. The personal costs of activism are high and some women, quite understandably, make the choice to focus solely on their family's survival under austerity. However, our interviews also indicate that other women seek to subvert their precarity, by using it as a springboard for organising and mobilising in their community.

Activism as self-help, self-care and self-organising

Sara Ahmed has reflected powerfully on self-care as warfare and we would like to begin here with her experiences, and the wisdom she draws from Audre Lorde:

'Caring for myself is not self-indulgence, it is self-preservation, and that is an act of political warfare.'
This is a revolutionary, extraordinary sentence. It is a much-loved, much-cited sentence. It is an arrow, which acquires its sharpness from its own direction. It is from the epilogue to Audre Lorde's *A Burst of Light*, a piece of writing so profound, so moving, that it never fails to teach me, often by leaving me undone, beside myself. This writing is made up of fragments or notes put together as Audre Lorde

learns that she has liver cancer, that her death could only be arrested; as she comes to feel that diagnosis in her bones. The expression 'a burst of light' is used for when she came to feel the fragility of her body's situation: 'that inescapable knowledge, in the bone, of my own physical limitation'.

A Burst of Light is an account of how the struggle for survival is a life struggle and a political struggle. Some of us, Audre Lorde notes were never meant to survive. To have some body, to be a member of some group, to be some, can be a death sentence. When you are not supposed to live, as you are, where you are, with whom you are with, then survival is a radical action; a refusal not to exist until the very end; a refusal not to exist until you do not exist. We have to work out how to survive in a system that decides life for some requires the death or removal of others. Sometimes: to survive in a system is to survive a system. We can be inventive, we have to be inventive, Audre Lorde suggests, to survive.

Some of us.

Others: not so much. (Ahmed 2014)

Self-help, self-care and self-organising are complementary and alternative spaces and an important source of personal support, resilience, information and community beyond the white-dominated, politically raceless, anti-austerity spaces that we critique in Chapter Two. However, at the same time they are not completely impervious to some of the same 'enterprising' challenges faced by third sector organisations and workers, who are often at the same time activists in grassroots spaces.

For one minority woman activist and third sector worker in Edinburgh, because of the pressures on women through a reduced and now punitive welfare state, personal relationships and solidarities that begin within third sector organisations become stronger and transcend them, turning into DIY autonomous spaces in which survival is a radical action:

> 'The pressures are higher on women to get out of the welfare system ... I think they are talking to each other a lot more about how they're managing financially or managing their goals and ambitions ... I think they are discussing ways within our women's group as well as to how to collectively manage but it's just a few of them, it's not like a movement

or anything, it depends on their personal relationship with the other women that they come into contact with, and how much do they like each other, how much they trust each other, but I don't think there is anything organised that has come out of this as yet … I think they're finding ways of connecting with each other which go beyond just mere gossip, it's about ways of supporting and surviving, because they know that this state which until recently took on a lot more responsibility of helping them to grow, is reducing its role, or is changing its role where earlier it was about helping people heal, now it's about getting them into work, of course what sort of work when there's no jobs and even the work that they are being directed to is not ambitious enough, it doesn't necessarily consider the cultural implications because to tell a woman who experiences domestic abuse that the only option you have because of your colour of your skin, the qualifications you have, the fact that you can't speak English, all of these things, is you become a cleaner, that's somehow the only option they are being shown or you become a care worker and there is nothing else more creative being shown to them. So I think when they speak to each other they are beginning to dream a little bit more, have a lot more ambition and finding ways of working together.' (Participant SC11)

In some cases, a feeling of powerlessness then catalysed self-help initiatives and lead to new collectives and social alliances (Ahmed 2004). As an activist migrant woman in Glasgow explained:

'I think there is need as part of our work to acknowledge where our efforts can stop and not really be in this room dreaming about things that we can't actually change, and therefore if our focus can be on improving the way we feel, improving our health and wellbeing, you know the sort of soft outcomes that we can work on then eventually maybe once we are in a better position we can begin to look at the bigger challenges.' (Participant SC12)

The severity of the cuts acts as a double-edged sword, according to the Black activist in London quoted earlier. The 'tyrant-type bosses' who this participant denounces, the insecure employment, the precariousness as a single parent, a Black woman working two jobs with unsociable shifts, will nonetheless lead to a politics of survival of a system, 'because of how high the stakes are stacked against us'. She identified the ways in which these tough times galvanise minority women to action:

> 'I've also seen Black women who were not activists before now involved because of how high the stakes are against us, stacked up against us, and what we're encountering, that it's forced them to become active, so there's that aspect of it as well.' (Participant EN7)

Hill Collins (2000: 201) reminds us that survival as a form of resistance is the legacy of Black women's struggle, it forms the foundations of Black women's activism, and is also the struggle to provide for the survival of children. Here, 'to survive in a system is to survive a system', as Lorde and Ahmed so powerfully demonstrate (Ahmed 2014).

The 'system' to be resisted is also the system of border control. Migrant networks have long undertaken informal grassroots action to share information and create networks of self-help, as this participant noted in Glasgow:

> 'As funding has disappeared and some groups have dissolved as a result of that, more informal groupings are emerging and definitely for some particular groups, some migrant groups particularly they are setting up more informal self-help and on a very grassroots basis, not necessarily with any funding but it quite often starts with somebody finds out something and then through word of mouth various people get together and then set up groupings that way.' (Participant SC13)

Across all sites of our research, minority women have formed groups that do not seek funding, so they avoid some of the pitfalls of enterprise in the third sector explored in the previous chapter and instead focus on supporting each other – a radical politics of self-care and survival. A Scottish Chinese woman in Glasgow discussed how, in spite of the cuts, her local group continues to meet and socialise, mostly through the self-help efforts of the group members:

> 'I go to a women's group, it is actually a women's and carers group, so anybody who cares for children are allowed to go. It is through the school. We are still running, but they

have cut back. We used to do things like yoga and Tai Chi therapy and lots of different courses. But the funding for them has gone, so now we teach each other. So I teach people how to crochet. Somebody teaches us how to knit. Somebody teaches us how to sew. We get people in to discuss the benefits.' (CRER Participant 3)

This politics of survival and self-care extends an ethic of care to create new affective networks of solidarity and support. While it also holds the potential to equip women with knowledge to combat the savagery of a punitive benefits system, its guiding ethos is care and support: this is survival as a radical action in and of itself.

While existing outside of often white-dominated politically raceless spaces, some alliances were possible with third sector organisations on careful, respectful terms:

'There are small women's groups out there and these women coming together and most of them actually we are working with so what we try is we'll go along and meet them. Either at somebody's house or it could be local Children's Centre we'll go and meet the women. And one example of that is [...] Refugee Centre, they have a women's group in [...] and it's more a friendship group and it's you know women get together and they do arts and crafts and we go and work, we will go and raise awareness whatever it happens to be. Whether it's going to talk about cancer, if they're pregnant we'll talk about [...] programme and engage them onto that, so there are pockets of women and still for those women is so crucial that they have a women only group that they can go to.' (Participant EN8)

When funding was sought, it took its toll on the applicants, indicating that even these grassroots spaces are not impervious to the challenges of 'enterprise':

'We formed a group. I know there is funding there, but you need the people to volunteer to do the work. We were a group with committee members ... we are keeping the group, but we are not going to have the committee ... No structure. Because nobody wants to be Treasurer, nobody wants to be Secretary, nobody wants to be the Chair person. Which means that ... there will be even less funding, you know. We can't apply for a lot of funding. If you are a group you can apply for funding.' (CRER Participant 4)

In this woman's view, people just do not have the time and are scared of the amount of work that formalising and professionalising an informal network might entail. Echoing Janet Newman's (2013) observations about feminist projects under austerity more broadly, our participant in Glasgow explains:

'So this is the problem with these groups. That's why at the schools, the committee groups are all poorly attended. It is always the same parents who volunteer for the things. You will find that at church groups as well.' (CRER Participant 4)

Furthermore, these self-help networks and groups are not without their own gendered power dynamics where, in one case, a man was identified as actually leading women's groups and blocking engagement with the third sector worker interviewed. This was perceived as particularly problematic in cases of domestic violence, where:

'the police will go to him first and ask him to go with them to the person's home... [and the man will] say 'that's not how we do it here' which is a quote, it's just appalling. So there are instance when we do get back to the barrier.' (Participant EN8)

In France, a South American woman working with migrant women who she saw as 'victims' of violence emphasised the challenges faced by 'small' associations that do good work and then disappear, as they are the true innovators:

'They are more responsive because they are rooted in the local context. So of course they are much more responsive than the state. What is important is to give to these associations, these little structures [the chance] to create actions, to experiment, to see what works. This enriches the social fabric, develops networks of solidarity, exactly what we need right now to get through this difficult period and not the state which creates these massive elephants ... these dinosaurs, these huge structures that at a certain moment become so dependent on state funding that it is difficult for them to play a role as a counter power … this creates a relationship of dependence.' (Participant FR12)

New solidarities are created, yet these are the same grassroots spaces where creative juices are being sucked dry, and the small associations then disappear due to the predatory enterprise culture we discussed in Chapter Four. The politics of survival is fragile for the collective as well as for the individual, and these grassroots spaces are both a site of depletion and resistance.

Activism as self-representation?

Participants in our research in grassroots organisations in both 'multicultural' England and 'republican' France felt misrepresented. In England, some women's umbrella groups positioned themselves as representing migrant and minority women in problematic ways. While they sometimes identified these limitations themselves, they still continued with their mobilisation:

> 'It's harder to raise the voices of the women in the community who are not going to turn up at a Reclaim the Night [National women-only march against sexual violence and for gender equality] … for example University students around sexual harassment, [it is] a huge problem for University students at the moment, well always has been. But in terms of women in the community the issues they face might not be, if they pick up a leaflet say for Reclaim the Night that might not be appropriate for them, they might not see, and their immediate problem might be paying the rent, feeding their children, going to the Food Bank … So by association women will be benefitting 'cause if suddenly women's issues are on the agenda then women in the community they're having voice through that platform but it might not be their voices that we're hearing if that makes sense?' (Participant EN8)

Our interviews in France provided a particularly rich insight into battles over representation.

Battles between movements such as *Ni Putes Ni Soumises* (NPNS) [literally Neither Whores Nor Submissive] and *Mouvement des Indigenes de la République* [Movement of the Indigenous of the Republic] are well known and widely mediatised in France. NPNS has mobilised against violence against women in the troubled suburbs of France. This movement is largely made up of women 'of immigrant origin', who live in difficult social and economic conditions in housing estates across France. These women have long protested against the gendered forms of violence they have endured at the hands of men within their communities. For example, in 2002, Sohane Benziane was burnt to death near her home in Vitry sur Seine in the Parisian suburbs, and other young women have been gang-raped, all of which has been well publicised through autobiographical texts. Leaders of this movement – including Fadela Amara, who was Secretary of State in charge of Urban Policy (Politique de la Ville) (2007-2010) – oppose the headscarf, which is 'an intolerable form of discrimination against women' (Ni Putes Ni Soumises 2005).

Women within this movement and others advancing similar positions in France have been highly audible (Bassel 2012). Fernando notes that they[2] 'all claim to be ideally suited to speak on behalf of their sisters silenced by patriarchal Islamic *intégristes*, and all have achieved levels of political success and media saturation unprecedented for women of colour in France' (Fernando 2013: 151).

Other actors have mobilised to create a counternarrative, in which it is possible to speak and to be heard on different terms. For example, *Mouvement des Indigènes de la République* was created in 2005 following the passage of the 2004 law banning religious signs in state schools, described in the movement's founding declaration as 'Discriminatory, sexist and racist, the anti-headscarf law is a colonial law of exception' (Indigènes de la République, 2005). Members include public intellectuals, activists and French youth of African, North African and Caribbean origin, born and raised in France. It then became a political party (from February 2010). The aim of the *Indigènes* is to denounce the instrumentalisation of women and women's bodies. They argue that the 2004 law is a neocolonial measure in a France that 'was a colonial state and remains a colonial state', and they have decried the 'colonial continuum' that composes the French social order (Indigènes de la République, 2005). The same Muslims who were told under colonial occupation to integrate on republican terms in Algeria are now being asked to do the same in France; they are protesting to demand acceptance as Muslims and as full citizens, a claim as unacceptable to the French government today as it was to the French colonial authorities then (Delphy, 2005, in Bowen, 2007: 216) (Bassel 2014).

For the *Indigènes*, the legacy of French colonial domination flows in a continuous line to the present. A founding member and spokesperson, Houria Bouteldja, draws a straight line from the unveiling ceremony in

Algiers in 1958 to *Ni Putes Ni Soumises* (Bouteldja 2004). By crossing temporal boundaries, they make hitherto unspeakable connections across time as well as place.[3] This challenge has not been made across the social divisions of the here and now – as was the case in the 1980s with 'universal' French anti-racist movements such as *SOS Racisme* – but across time and within the divisions and inequalities that are named as the legacy of colonialism.[4] This is an important challenge to the grammar of the universal Republic and the social order it legitimises (Bassel 2014).

The *Indigènes* contrast their actions not only with *Ni Putes Ni Soumises* but also with the anti-racist movements of the 1980s, including the '*mouvement beur*'[5] – the ambitious social project aiming to capitalise on the liberalisation of the law on associations in 1981, before which foreigners' rights to be involved in French politics were negligible (Bassel and Lloyd 2011).[6] This movement involved young people of Maghrebi origins, many of whom were French citizens, who challenged earlier forms of migrant organising in order to mobilise the 'second generation'. They campaigned locally against discriminatory policing and racist violence, and asserted 'the right to exist and express a double and contradictory identity, without proclaiming allegiance to a defined national group' (Wihtol de Wenden and Leveau, 2001: 26). A series of marches through France channelled the ferment of revolt and creativity among young people, involving them in theatre groups, free radios, innovative demonstrations and solidarity activities, which coalesced along the staging posts. The first *Marche pour l'égalité et contre le racisme* ('March for equality and against racism') drew a considerable amount of media attention, and the leaders found themselves wooed by the ruling *Parti Socialiste*. Over time, leaders became media personalities, and some elements were co-opted by mainstream political parties, gaining funding but losing their cutting edge and connection to the grassroots. This mobilisation had mixed results. It is viewed by many, not only by the *Indigènes*, as a *mouvement avorté*, an 'aborted movement', in which even the term '*beur*' is appropriated and interpreted exclusively as a rupture with the culture of the parents, denying the claim to identity and memory of one's origins and the emergence of a multicultural, urban identity (Bouamama, 1994).

Co-optation and being instrumentalised

The legacy of this 'aborted' struggle for minority women activists in the *milieu associatif* (the field of civil society organisations) is twofold.

First, for critics the *milieu associatif* is arguably a sphere of co-optation rather than emancipation. Minority women's grassroots activism is predominantly framed and legitimised as 'go betweens', as *femmes relais* (literally 'relay women', or interpreters, intercultural mediators and intermediaries), who 'translate' and 'communicate' community issues to state actors, continuing the appropriation of women's often lower profile and grassroots activism in the *mouvement beur*. This role was recognised since the 1980s,[7] and then became increasingly professionalised.[8] Over the decades, these women have intervened in a wide range of social issues, including access to education and health services, youth crime prevention, poor housing, unemployment and welcoming new arrivals to France (Bouadbillah 1997).[9] However, with the professionalisation of the *femmes relais*, and that of 'socio-cultural mediator' (Barthélémy 2009), comes the problem of appropriation. Those minority women working in these roles may experience a loss of independence, especially when they seek government funding (Poinsot 2001). Issues of appropriation may become exacerbated as *femmes relais* negotiate the changing terrain of the *milieu associatif* in terms of funding cuts and the enterprise culture that we identified in the previous chapter. Furthermore, the role of transmitting information between two parties does not necessarily involve the ability to make different kinds of proposals, to critique government policy or to refuse and subvert the process of consultation altogether (Delcroix 1997: 52-4). Thus, the formal recognition of *femmes relais* arguably 'chilled' other forms of minority women's activism in the *milieu* and, perhaps unintentionally, has produced a form of grassroots action and dialogical relations with the state that can be difficult to refuse.

Second, minority women have also been instrumentalised through the reproduction of the Republican frame of saving women in the *cités* (the troubled housing estates) from the men in their communities. This was the case for some of the young women involved in *Ni Putes Ni Soumises*, who were dressed up as *Mariannes de la République* and photographed wearing the revolutionary Phrygian cap. The photos were shown on the pillars of the National Assembly, marking how their cause was embraced by the political elite.[10] As Mariam Ticktin describes it:

> we are left with the question of how to recognize the very real violence that the founding members of NPNS ... endured; the question becomes how they can speak their violence without being effectively silenced or co-opted by nationalist or postcolonial projects. By being rendered

audible only through stereotypes, survivors of violence are
silenced as subjects and as anything else other than victims.
(Ticktin 2008: 884)

Negotiating the Republic

In our study, some minority women activists adopted a Republican line,
warning against the dangers of *communautarisme* (this term reflects the
fear in France of 'communities' leading to segregation and ghettoes) and
so-called 'identity politics'. However, at the same time they demanded
that the French state recognise their political agency, particularly as
defenders of other minority women who were 'victims' of violence. (In
one case, a participant encouraged the women with whom she worked
to remove body covering, a process she referred to as 'unveiling', as
an act of saving them from violence.) In these cases, there was often
a feeling of some minority women being 'spoken for', rather than
listened to. Despite what these women felt were their powerful social
and political interventions, they were not being recognised as political
actors. They are instrumentalised, treated as means toward the ends of
the Republic, rather than recognised as political equals.

One minority woman activist in our research (whose organisation
worked with women from a specific ethnic group as well as the
general public, focusing on survivors of violence, and which no longer
exists due to funding being withdrawn) described her experience of
being instrumentalised. She maintained high professional standards in
providing services to vulnerable migrant and minority women, and
chose to invest in well-maintained facilities and highly qualified staff.
Her competence and professionalism were met with a hostile reception
from public authorities:

> 'I always explained to the state that an association working
> with migrants, with women … it should not be a pigsty. The
> way *étrangers* are received, women in the *quartiers*, exactly
> Madame Amara in the damn *quartiers sensibles* [sensitive
> areas, the ZUS of Chapter Three], in facilities that are made
> available to associations with disgusting toilets and not even
> soap to wash your hands … this is not respecting people and
> I always said if I work in the *associatif* it is to respect people
> … How many times did I have French political officials
> who came to the association and "oh, it's chic here". Wait
> a minute, "chic"? It's *clean* … It's terrible to explain the
> mentality to you. [The participants' association] became

bothersome/a problem [*genante*] because, I almost want to say, it was too well kept and maybe too professional.' (Participant FR7)

Participant FR7 described a 'false democracy': a 'double game' was played, where funding was provided but then withdrawn, ostensibly on the grounds of fairness (though in fact because of disagreement with the way work was being done, despite her general adherence and endorsement of Republican, secular norms). The argument of 'fairness' was advanced through government officials asking why other associations working with specific groups of migrant and minority women did not work as well as she did. At the same time, she was told that she could not be given more funding, as this would be unfair to the others – a policy she referred to as a race to the bottom [*nivellement vers le bas*]. Generally, in her view, the economic crisis was an excuse to justify political choices and to control her activism – and the activism of others in the associative milieu.

Other participants positioned themselves outside the Republican frame altogether, but acknowledged the ways in which they were nonetheless constrained in what they could say. For example, in one case a white activist explained that in terms of the law, she and her group could no longer use the term 'state racism' [*racisme d'état*] because:

> 'It's a defamatory term and so if we use it we can be prosecuted … We have resigned ourselves to what other associations use, the other associations said "avoid using the term 'state racism', you can say 'xenophobia'" … it is more of a recommendation, they recommend we not use it because we can be prosecuted, this comes from the legal teams, so we changed it.' (Participant FR11)

However, this is the only form of censorship she has experienced. Her South American colleague reflected on the lack of recognition of difference, and what this means for migrant women particularly. She spoke with sensitivity about how they work with migrant women who are victims of violence, demonstrating awareness of the challenges migrant women face at the intersections of multiple forms of oppression:

> 'We are very careful at [her organisation] because we defend the rights of *étrangers* and migrants and we don't want to stigmatise, it is not about treating violence against migrant

women with the idea that migrant men are violent, that is the danger, and we try not to fall into this discourse.' (Participant FR13)

Instead, all women should be protected. This reflexivity – and the intersectional politics that results – can by no means be assumed, as we see in the contrast with the examples discussed earlier. Personal narratives and political strategies of survival are enmeshed in and/or against Republican ideology, and interact with the effects of austerity. We need to question the limits of this sensitive and intersectional politics when, at the same time, Participant FR13's colleague (Participant FR11) explains that 'state racism' cannot be named.

Speaking against stigma and naming intersections

A different discourse emanates from Blanc-Mesnil, a district located in the Seine-Saint-Denis department of France. It is portrayed by the media, by politicians and in the popular imagination as an infamous site of disorder and failure. The women of the *quartiers populaires* [working class neighbourhoods] of Blanc-Mesnil do not use the language of 'race' in their fascinating political statement, made in a book with sociologist Saïd Bouamama. Yet they speak intersectionally against the stigmatisation of their young people, their area, their own identities and the distortion of their voices (see further discussion in Bassel, forthcoming). They organised as a collective, outside the professional white Left, and published the book *Femmes des quartiers populaires. En résistance contre les discriminations* [Women from working class neighbourhoods. In resistance against discriminations] (Bouamama and Femmes du Blanc-Mesnil 2013) to speak for themselves, because:

> Many people speak about us … We worked on this book because we wanted to speak ourselves about our life, our situation, our difficulties. No one knows better than us what we are living. No one knows better the situation of the *quartiers populaires*. *La parole* [voice] has to come back to those who concretely live the situation of *popular quarters*. We don't want to wait to be given *la parole*. We wanted to simply take it. (Bouamama and Femmes du Blanc-Mesnil 2013: 200)

They identify a triple penalty that they face: 'The first is being from *milieu populaires* ['working class backgrounds and areas']. The second is to be of immigrant background. And the third is to live in Seine-Saint-Denis' (Bouamama and Femmes du Blanc-Mesnil 2013: 115). The discourse of elite actors, both in mainstream media and by politicians, has characterised them as 'dirty', as 'savages' and in the infamous words of former president Sarkozy as 'scum' [*racaille*], to be cleaned with a water cannon:

> Our lives are already violent enough for us not to be further insulted ... This violence of words that we experience does a lot of damage. It hurts our dignity and barbarises us. The cup is overflowing. We can't take it anymore. We expect politicians to attend to real problems rather than. The problem of this society is poverty, unemployment and racist discrimination and not young people, the *quartiers* ['dangerous areas'], immigration. It is not only the young people who were in revolt in November 2005 who are enraged. We also can't take it anymore, even if we don't express it the same way. (Bouamama and Femmes du Blanc-Mesnil 2013: 180-1)

They name their politics of survival in this context:

> When we say 'us', we are speaking about the women of the *quartiers populaires*. As it is often women who carry on their shoulders the consequences of poverty that affect *familles populaires* [working-class families]. It is the women who ask the question of survival everyday with lower and lower incomes. It is the women who are in the front line of difficulties with children whether it is in school or when they look for a job. Yes, women of the *quartiers populaires* are in the front line ... in all areas. We want to shout '*vive les femmes*' [long live women] as we have suffered and will still suffer. (Bouamama and Femmes du Blanc-Mesnil 2013: 200-1)

They 'survive the system' through their book as a collective, creative act, which extends beyond the pages to strengthen existing solidarities – with local politicians and activists – and to reach a broader audience. The white Left typically dismisses women from this part of France as apolitical victims and failed mothers of 'scum', while nonetheless claiming to defend class politics and wealth redistribution in the name of the 'universal' working class. Instead of waiting for recognition from the Left, these women take *la parole* and authorise their own actions, asserting their politics of survival as a radical act.

Social movements

Our research was undertaken until May 2014, before several key groups were well-established and became active. These now include: in England, Sisters Uncut (who take direct action in defense of anti-violence against women services), Focus EC15 (a mothers' group campaigning for 'social housing not social cleansing' in London) and Sisters of Frida (an experimental collective of disabled women); and in France, Mwasi Collectif (discussed in Chapter 6), Intersectionalité TMTC and Ferguson in Paris. Therefore we caught a moment in which activists identified a vacuum, which has since begun to be filled by new groups that merit their own study to explore the ways in which they are led and made by and with minority women.

In our study, this gap was identified by one of our participants, the Black activist in England quoted earlier, who argues that the structure of anti-austerity social movements excludes minority women's concerns from the outset. She reported experiences of racism *and* sexism in the articulation of claims and in the representation of activists in these ostensibly radical spaces:

> 'From the perspective of Black women who perhaps are political, who do want to campaign … if they look at the face of the anti-cuts movement and see it's quite male-dominated that may put them off getting involved, may not give them the confidence to get involved and just because it's an anti-cuts movement doesn't mean to say there's not racism within it.' (Participant EN7)

In this participant's view, there is a particular category of white activists to whom:

> 'You have to explain it and spell it out to them. Now these are supposed to be people that are supposed to understand the history … about the context, about what true equality means and what oppression is, and they will say they know that and they will give you all the good headlines or put the good quotes out there but the reality is they don't really understand it because otherwise you wouldn't have to remind them over and over again, and you wouldn't have

to spell it out, so it is quite a struggle, it's quite tough …
They get very defensive because they don't want to actually
admit they've got it wrong.' (Participant EN7)

It is for future research to assess the extent to which these new minority
women-led, anti-austerity groups have 'got it right'. We will return
to explore these new movements in the next chapter.

Conclusion

In this chapter, we have reflected on minority women activists' personal
narratives and how they speak about and construct their DIY activist
spaces. These spaces stand in direct contrast to the politically raceless
discussions of the white Left, which often seeks to deny and erase
intersectional perspectives and activism. We have explored minority
activism and its connections to third sector spaces and argued that
minority women's activism should not be dismissed or ignored because
of the links to this sector. As we discussed in Chapter Two, minority
women's activism is misrecognised, because it does not fit with the
hegemonic constructions of what 'politics' and 'activism' are supposed
to be under a framework of white ignorance. As we have demonstrated
in this chapter, minority women are radical activists simply *because*
they are survivors. Their politics of survival represents a challenge to
dominant ideas of what constitutes activism and the exclusivity of some
variants of social movement theory which do not name these spaces.

When minority women's activist spaces are misrecognised or erased
by white Left activists, and self-care is not understood as political
warfare, then solidarity cannot be built between activists. We demand
that minority women be seen as radical agents, who authorise their
own actions rather than waiting for legitimacy from the white Left.

In Chapter Six, we will reflect on what we can learn about minority
women's activism across our case studies.

Notes
[1] See Lorde 1988.
[2] She provides the examples of women like Amara and Chahdortt Djavann (an
Iranian dissident and writer).
[3] The title of the movement names a vital, invisible link between the *Code de
l'Indigénat* (the 'Code of the Indiginate') , first in effect in Algeria in 1881 and
revoked in 1946, the 'juridical monster' of state racism exported from Algeria
throughout the territories of the Empire during colonial expansion (Barkat 2005;
Le Cour Grandmaison 2010) that gave colonised people a subordinate, racialised

status, and the 'universal' Republic which served as a justification for colonialism (Pereira 2010: 172).

4   The *Indigènes* have a broader political project of decolonial government and 'global' reform that reaches beyond French borders and denounces the United States, the European Union and the state of Israel as 'the main political centres where global colonial domination resides' (Indigènes de la République 2010).

5   'Beur' is simply a term initially used by young people to describe themselves, derived from the *verlan* (backslang) for *Arabe*. It became associated with a rather patronising, co-option of the movement and was shunned by the more radical tendencies.

6   Bouadbillah 1997; this and the next paragraph draw on Bassel and Lloyd 2011.

7   See: Cohen-Emerique 1993; Delcroix 1995; Quiminal et al 1995; Bouadbillah 1997; Delcroix 1997; Mendoza 1997; Quiminal 1997; Veith 2000; Dugué and Rist 2002; Merckling 2002; Minces 2006; Le Monde 2006.

8   The *adultes-relais* programme ('*adultes-relais* refer to male or female intercultural mediators) was adopted by the *Conseil national des villes* ('National Council of Cities') in 1999 and became operational at the end of 2000 (Barthélémy 2009). At this time, the term 'socio-cultural mediator' was formalised (Dugué and Rist 2002).

9   See also Delcroix 1995, Bentchicou 1997, Dugué and Rist 2002.

10 For a statement from the National Assembly, which notes that the 'Mariannes' themselves identify the Republic as the best protection for women of all origins, see: www.assemblee-nationale.fr/evenements/mariannes.asp

SIX

Learning across cases, learning beyond 'cases'

The road we have travelled

We began our empirical analysis by arguing that the policy frame of the 2008 economic crisis further erases minority women's precarity by focusing policy attention and resources on the exceptional experiences of the economically privileged.

In Chapter Three, we demonstrated how minority women's routinised crises – institutionalised, ordinary and everyday social and economic inequalities – are treated as unremarkable in policy and political discourses, until minority groups disrupt the social order.

In Chapter Four, we then considered how third sector organisations are sites of minority women's activism, and explored what happens when these organisations become objects of state policy through governance arrangements and the impact this has on minority women's activism. In ostensibly opposite contexts of 'multicultural' Scotland and England and 'republican' France, we find similar issues at play. In a context of third sector organisations' cut-throat relationships with each other, and where practitioners are disciplined into neoliberal ways of working, there appear to be rapidly shrinking spaces in which minority women activists articulate and advance their intersectional social justice claims.

Finally, in Chapter Five, we reflected on minority women activists' personal narratives and how they speak about and construct their DIY activist spaces. These spaces stand in direct contrast to the politically raceless discussions of the white Left, which often seeks to deny and erase intersectional perspectives and activism. Minority women are radical activists simply *because* they are survivors. Their politics of survival represents a challenge to dominant ideas of what constitutes activism.

In this chapter, we take a step back to think across these three cases, and 'beyond' them. In the first section, we reflect on our cases in order to avoid the analytical straightjacket of national 'models' that can obscure similarities as much as they also elucidate differences.

In the second section, we move 'beyond' these cases, in the sense of thinking about the internationalist and autonomous dimensions of intersectional and minority women-led organising that we see in the creative, subversive and influential voices and actions of new actors and movements in both France and Britain.

Learning across cases: state power and national 'models'

The 'multicultural' and 'republican' national 'models' of citizenship derived from France and Britain's colonial adventures have figured throughout this book and undeniably influence minority women's activism and their politics of survival. However, their effects are unpredictable and inconstant. Indeed, minority women's experiences can also lead us to question the coherence and totality of what are often presented as comprehensive national 'models'.

Our attempt to learn across cases echoes the well-established literature that questions the existence of overly schematic 'models' and how they generate particular knowledge about the exercise of state power. Rather than illuminating state action, these models of state power have been described by some scholars as belonging to a handful of 'loosely connected syndromes' (Freeman 2004), 'tenacious stereotypes' (Lloyd 1995) and 'extremely attractive, but limited, narratives' (Bertossi et al 2015: 74). Some scholars point instead to the convergence of policies towards the restriction of minority rights and a retreat from multiculturalism (Joppke 2007a, 2007b).

There is a fine line to walk, however, as these 'models' cannot simply be dismissed either. As Christophe Bertossi et al (2015: 73-4) suggest, they matter because social actors believe in their existence. While 'models' undeniably contain institutional inconsistencies, normative incoherence, uneven distribution and contested meanings, the model concepts 'are used, imagined, negotiated, affirmed, contested, and challenged by different types of individual and collective actors in very different settings'. We analyse these contestations, affirmations and negotiations from a neglected vantage point: that of minority women *activists*, not victims, who draw on – as well as reject and mobilise against– the normative frameworks and promises that the respective national 'models' and exercises of state power provide.

The 'strong' French Jacobin state with its highly centralised government powers; the rise of left-wing nationalism in 'multicultural' Scotland and its (debatable) commitment to social democracy; and the localism agenda in England – all have posited certain promises for minority women:

- republican emancipation and protection *from* culture and community and the protection of the *Etat providence* [welfare state] in France;
- social inclusion and multicultural progressive politics in an independent Scotland;
- freedom to 'get on' with grassroots work away from the bureaucracy and constraint of the local and national state in England.

Yet in the experiences of our participants, the state is strong in different ways that also constrain political possibilities in unexpected ways. Minority women's experiences of state power are not always consistent with the template that 'models' provide us with, and instead they must negotiate contradictory moments.

Learning across cases from the perspective of minority women activists challenges the portrayal of the enabling multicultural Scottish and English states in contrast to the omnipresent and dominant French Republican state. It demonstrates instead the constraints of measures such as the 'gagging bill' and the localism agenda under the 2010 Coalition government in the UK and the simultaneous withdrawal and intervention of the Republican state in France.

State as trusted interlocutor?

In France, as discussed in the previous chapter, the colonial legacy has until recently been unspeakable, although it has been very publicly denounced by movements such as *Indigènes de la République*. Several minority women activists in our study conceived of the state in 'colour-blind' terms, as the powerful *Etat-providence* [welfare state]:

> 'Does the state need associations, yes or no? If it needs them, how does it give them real and concrete resources so they can do properly what they are asked to do? If the state does not need associations, in that case, they have to stop *brasser du vent* [blowing hot air], they should say so right away and these associations have to turn to other things.' (Participant FR10)

For many participants, the state should be the main interlocutor, the main power broker. It is even beyond certain forms of critique because of its power; it is not possible to name state racism, as we saw in Chapter Five, for fear of legal proceedings. There is a particular cultural status and history of relationship between the state and the *milieu associatif* (see Chapter One and Chapter Four), in which there persists an expectation and a hope of the state: as a core funder, a moral guarantor and a protector of *droits communs* [common/shared rights] that should not be interfered with by the free market:

Interviewer: 'And these are *droits communs?*'
Participant: 'Yes *voilà*, and for us it is important not to confuse the two [the state and the market]. So then to ask first for private money [fundraising] that only enters very recently into French culture.' (Participant FR3)

Participant FR3 goes on to explain that the 'social sector' is to be supported by the state, not private initiatives:

'[In France] there is a lot of confusion between the *secteur caritatif* [the third/charitable sector] whose origin was in charity and the sector of professional social action which has nothing to do with charity, it is solidarity.' (Participant FR3)

However, as we have seen in preceding chapters, this faith is slowly being eroded with the introduction of a free market logic to the third sector that generates political challenges for minority women's activism that we have documented throughout this book. The 'model' of a strong centralised Jacobin state is questionable in activists' own experiences when *l'Etat* is no longer an *Etat providence* [welfare state] and is neither present nor protective. Funding is withdrawn or a site of conflict and competition, with profound impacts on service provision, organising and solidarity, creating new forms of precarity and vulnerability for minority women. Yet, at the same time, the racial Republican state claims to 'save' minority women victims, on its own politically raceless, 'colour-blind' terms. Minority women activists must negotiate this contradiction.

State as censor

The disappointment and failed expectations of the state among participants in France are in sharp contrast to the social enterprise-driven culture of the English and Scottish cases, where there is an assumption that austerity will continue, that the state will not protect them and that the market will continue to dominate and be the master to be served.

However, participants in England identified deeply problematic exercises of state power that were akin to the prohibition of naming 'state racism' in France: this was the 'gagging bill', officially known as the 'Transparency of Lobbying, Non-party Campaigning and Trade Union Administration Act 2014'. The Act has a number of aims, including the closer regulation of election campaign spending by those not standing for election or registered as political parties.[1] It faced widespread criticism and opposition, particularly from third sector organisations, who feared it could limit freedom of speech in the run-up to an election, and was branded the 'gagging bill' because of the restrictions it would put on how much third sector organisations can spend while campaigning on non-partisan political issues before an election.

Liz Hutchins, senior campaigner at Friends of the Earth, claimed the day the Act was passed to be a 'bad day for anyone wanting to protect the environment, save a hospital or oppose tuition fees' (The Guardian 2014). Sir Stephen Bubb, chief executive of the Association of Chief Executives of Voluntary Organisations (ACEVO) directly challenged the chilling effect on political action in the third sector: 'We must be clear: civil society must never lose its voice. We must stand up for our beliefs and refuse self-censorship. ACEVO will work tirelessly to ensure that this Bill does not gag charities and campaigners' (The Guardian 2014).

We observed the chilling effects of the Act on minority women activists in England. Activists reported reluctance on the part of larger charities, acting as sponsoring organisations, that would no longer allow their names to be mentioned in association with minority women-led projects. These were perceived to be 'partisan' and political, even though the aims were about citizenship rights – for example, aiming to promote participation in politics in general, rather than support of a *particular* political party. Larger third sector organisations' reluctance to fund this sort of work was perceived to then lead to self-censorship among smaller, minority women-led initiatives, including those opposing austerity. In the words of this minority woman activist, who engaged directly in formal politics as well as grassroots initiatives:

> 'I think generally it is that larger organisations, charitable organisations ... they're not allowed to promote or support political ... ideas eighteen months in the run up to the general election which is just disgusting because it's, it is a gagging order ... It means a lot of work can't get done cause, yeah it's just, I'm just getting annoyed thinking about

it, sorry [laughs]. It's just … it's just very, very frustrating. And I think it's gonna have a huge impact, you know, next year [in the run up to the 2015 general election] as well. I mean it's already had a huge impact anyway but when, in the next twelve months it's gonna have, you know, a bigger impact…. I think in terms of like supporting causes, for example. So say, for example, that the bedroom taxes, they [minority women] wanna … campaign against it. They can't campaign against that … they're taking away the freedom of, you know, expression, freedom of right to, you know, protest and … Anything political orientated they cannot promote or support … Or even sending out … like a mailing list about it or anything. Cause that'll be seen to be, you know, supporting the campaign or whatnot … it's just that they can't say anything, you know.' (Participant EN9)

The censoring effects of state power directly impede minority women's activism across the two 'opposite' cases of 'difference-blind' France and 'multicultural' England, though in different ways. In France, the silencing effect of republican political racelessness does not allow the articulation of implicating the state as structurally racist, while simultaneously the state intervenes as a racial state to 'save' minority women from their 'backwards culture'. In 'multicultural' England, with its longstanding Black and minority ethnic third sector that is considered to be a site which enables minority activism, it is the attempt to curb third sector activism more generally (as well as that of trade unions) which then leads to self-censorship on the part of larger organisations. Larger organisations withdraw vital support from minority women-led initiatives, who in turn feel compelled to self-censor. The 'models', while present and 'active', are also 'absent' and belied by the different faces of state intervention that are experienced in 'chilling' ways by minority women.

State power as a centralised or local constraint?

'Models' are also threaded through experiences of different *levels* of state power in unpredictable ways. In France, several participants described the highly centralised and monolithic state that the 'model' would have us expect, unchanged by attempted decentralisation policies (and which we explored in some detail in previous chapters with respect to the Republican state's promise to 'emancipate' minority women yet it co-opts and instrumentalises minority women activists rather than treating them as political equals). In the words of one minority man:

> '[this is] the Jacobin aspect. This means that France, it [the centralised state] is everywhere ... [It is] a very particular political distribution. It is easier for a Deputy whose *commune* [the third tier of local government and administration in France, within *départements* and, in turn, the regions] is next to Paris to contact a minister directly than to contact a Prefect or someone else.' (Participant FR6)

In contrast, for our English participants, the local state was a significant feature of their experience, particularly with respect to the 'new' localism agenda, whereby the then Coalition government aimed:

> to both establish a 'Big Society' and put in place a localist reform agenda, specifically aimed at curbing the power of local authorities and opening up new spaces for community and private sector agencies. Three main methods have been deployed to secure this agenda: decentralization, transparency and providing finance. (Jacobs and Manzi 2013: 36)

The Localism Act 2011 was described by Greg Clark, Minister of State for Decentralisation at the time,[2] as 'the essence of the Big Society':

> We think that the best means of strengthening society is not for central government to try and seize all the power and responsibility for itself. It is to help people and their locally elected representatives to achieve their own ambitions. This is the essence of the Big Society.
>
> We have already begun to pass power back to where it belongs. We are cutting central targets on councils, easing the burden of inspection, and reducing red tape. We are breaking down the barriers that stop councils, local charities, social enterprises and voluntary groups getting things done for themselves.
>
> But we can go a lot further by changing the law. The Localism Act sets out a series of measures with the potential to achieve a substantial and lasting shift in power away from central government and towards local people. They include: new freedoms and flexibilities for local government; new

rights and powers for communities and individuals; reform to make the planning system more democratic and more effective, and reform to ensure that decisions about housing are taken locally. (Communities and Local Government 2011)[3]

Our research participants were skeptical, however, of these promises of the Big Society, particularly for minority women. When describing the ways in which they set up a third sector initiative for minority women, two of our participants (a minority man and woman) identify these changing relations to the local authority as well as the 'deficit' for minority women outside London as key challenges faced by their allies and partners. In responding to 'the agenda', which they described as being all about the Big Society and localism, they explain:

> Participant EN10: 'Austerity, localism ... I mean, we talk about a lot of the organisations that we trained, and exist now, and some of them don't exist, that had been funded by local authority for years and years and years, and had relied on that funding, had never really sought other areas of funding ... and that suddenly was under threat. So the nature of their whole organisation was under threat. Their service users, they were seeing an increased demand, there was things like domestic violence service providers, education and training service providers, so it was all about, "hang on a minute, this funding we've relied on for years is suddenly under threat, this means we're gonna have to make changes to our organisation". People were being encouraged to merge with each other, to, you know, think about new ways of funding, etcetera. And it was all new too, it was all new. Other organisations that ... have never had any funding, like, some quite active asylum seeker groups, like [names of groups] ... and they were much more about campaigning, because they didn't really run a service, so it didn't really make much difference to them, because they had nothing anyway.'

> Participant EN11: 'The issues are also about the regional aspect of the work. There's always been a, kind of a deficit, in relation to ethnic minority women's experiences outside of London.'

In Scotland, for one participant the problem was not the trend in Scottish and English social policy towards decentralisation and localism, but rather that this agenda masked massive cuts to the public and third sectors, which had a disproportionate impact on small community groups, especially minority women-led organisations:

> 'The localism agenda on its own right, in my view, is okay, but it doesn't work without resources being invested in it. You cannot assume that localism will work without money. Localism will work with money available to make things happen, and I think the other thing we should bear in mind is that small community groups are the ones that are dealing with individuals with very serious issues… They should have, for example, money for transport to be able to take a valuable client to the local Job Centre Plus so that they can be assessed for whatever reason or the other. Without that facility those community groups will not be able to assist that person. So…the localism agenda has to work with resources invested in it. To assume that it will work in a vacuum with no money is not going to work.' (Participant SC14)

The localism agenda and the Big Society held only a hollow promise for these minority women activists and their allies. Rather than 'breaking down the barriers that stop councils, local charities, social enterprises and voluntary groups getting things done for themselves', as suggested by Greg Clark above, these activists must face a shrinking pool of resources and a regulation of their political work. Rather than enabling, this reconfiguration of state power constrains activism.

The promise of independence?

In Scotland, at the time of our research, the relation to state power and the promise of the 'multicultural' model were also conditioned by the looming prospect of independence. Our fieldwork took place during the referendum campaign and for minority women activists who already felt vulnerable and hypervisible in Scotland, as we have discussed in previous chapters, the upcoming referendum vote further reinforced a feeling of powerlessness. The referendum was seen by some as a kind of shield for policy makers to hide behind to avoid addressing longstanding inequalities particularly affecting minority women:

'I think it's [the independence debate] making it much more difficult to have a genuine discussion because there is a sense that whatever you do will be pulled into a constitutional debate. There are other areas like for example childcare, which have been devolved to Scotland since devolution happened and yet you haven't seen any great movement on it.' (Participant SC1)

Limited powers under devolution could therefore serve as an excuse for inaction, even on issues for which the Scottish government has competence, with the following participant speculating that improving the living conditions of poor, minority women is not politically palatable:

'There's a child poverty strategy. There's a framework, the anti-poverty framework, and a solidarity target about reducing the inequality so everything's in place but they would argue that they can't do more until they've got more powers because of the welfare system not being within their power and they would argue that they've done what they can around passporting benefits etc, and all the rest of it, but genuinely in order for Alex Salmond [the then First Minister] to achieve his vision of a Scotland that he talks about, he would have to address poverty but I just wonder if it doesn't get the priority it does because it doesn't get a vote winner ... How do you make it palatable to a large swathe of ... Scotland and Scottish people which in some ways does a disservice to Scottish people because I do think that they tend to be a lot more progressive in their thinking than other parts of these isles. That's my diplomatic answer, just one of those awkward situations.' (Participant SC14)

Independence could, however, open up some political opportunities in fostering a greater sense of political responsibility and could make possible more radical spaces, especially for minority women's activism:

'I think one of the good things if we were to be independent is that it may ... encourage Scottish people to actually take more responsibility for who we do vote for because it would make a difference. Just now you can always sit back in terms of UK national stuff and go see it's the English that voted for them but really if we were governing our own country then we would have to start to take responsibility for the types of politicians that we voted in so you get what you're asking for, so I think that would make a difference and then we might be able to see policies that changed things more radically. Look at a different type of economic system or stuff like that. I think here about the different groups emerging like the Coalition for Resistance or the Occupy Movement and also broader globally like the transition movement or the Zeitgeist movement, then maybe we can see some of these things having an impact in our own country, we could manage that better.' (Participant SC14)

While the future landscape could open some opportunities for minority women, the Scottish independence campaign did not appear to enable genuine discussion about intersecting inequalities. Furthermore, the complexities of the devolution settlement served as an excuse to avoid potentially politically divisive issues that particularly impact on minority women, for example child poverty and affordable childcare. The relation to state power here is to a configuration in flux, and it is significant to note that respondents were not embracing the rhetoric of the progressive promise of independence, but were instead very realistically assessing the political opportunities in the Scottish landscape as they stood then. As in the previous chapter, we see here that political opportunities for minority women are more restricted than what the progressive Scottish rhetoric and 'model' suggest.

More generally, when the contestations, affirmations and negotiations of state 'models' are considered from the neglected vantage point of minority women activists, we see contradictions and inconsistencies in these supposed 'total' models of state action. While sometimes the models are drawn upon as normative resources, at other times their promises to provide, include and protect minority women are broken, while simultaneously 'saving' them, as we can see with the withdrawing and intervening French state. The enabling 'multicultural' Scottish and English states directly constrain activism through measures such as the 'gagging bill' and the effects of the localism agenda under the then Coalition government. Devolution serves as an excuse not to act or speak, and the promise of an independent Scotland is potentially radical but tenuous. State 'models' only partially reveal these exercises of state power and at other times do more to obscure than illuminate. Instead, when minority women's activism is the starting point, we see a landscape of contradiction that they must negotiate when determining whether and how to challenge state and market power. As we will now turn to examine, at some times and in some places, challenging the power of the state and the market can be done on minority women's own terms.

Learning beyond 'cases': new actors on the scene

Despite the very real barriers we have outlined in this chapter, new actors have emerged on the scene, presenting a ray of hope for anti-austerity and minority women's activism. As we began to discuss in the previous chapter, new minority women-led groups have emerged since our fieldwork was conducted, who name the intersectional challenges we have identified and place them at the heart of their action. Their struggles are important illustrations of resistance on terms that minority women set for themselves.[4]

In France, we deliberately turn our gaze away from the *Nuit Debout* movement which, as we argued in Chapter Five, is a further example of protest spaces dominated by white male voices and bodies that exclude minority women's analyses and interests. This is, simply put, the wrong place to look. Instead, we contend that the true possibilities lie in intersectional organising outside of the white Left, in movements such as the *Marche de la dignité*, which denounces police violence, places it at the heart of political debate and stages large protests. *Marche de la dignité* leaders are recognised in France as drawing on a range of traditions and legacies:

- the French *mouvement beur* (discussed in Chapter Five), specifically the *Marche pour l'égalité et contre le racisme* of 1983, which, as we noted, was subsequently appropriated by political elites;
- the memory of struggles in France around immigration since the 1980s;
- the '*émeutes*' (roughly translated as 'riots' or 'uprisings') of 2005 and their political legacy;
- here and now, Black Lives Matter as a global political force.

They speak in the name of all *minorités racialisés* [racialised minorities], a language that is already antithetical to the Republic, and claim their autonomy in these terms. As Nacira Guenif-Souilamas, a sociologist and movement member, states: 'We will make a declaration of independence from organisations of the left and the unions who have spoken in our name and confuse alliance with subordination' (Le Monde 2015).

The Mwasi Collectif[5] also claims autonomous space as a prerequisite and condition of political action. It is an Afrofeminist collective, created in 2014 by: '*Africaines* and *Afrodescendantes* who felt the need to come together, exchange and express ourselves on questions relating to Black Women' (Mwasi Collectif n.d.). It is a space exclusively for women and those assigned as 'women', who are Black and *métisses* [mixed heritage], to fight against racialised and gendered violence and different forms of oppression. They name the intersections of their struggles in many fields: class discrimination, gender, sexuality, health, religion and institutionalised heteropatriarchy (whereby men and heterosexuality have primacy over all others) in the white hegemonic capitalist system.

Marche de la dignité and the Mwasi Collectif are both internationalist movements, explicitly autonomous from the French Left and white French feminist movements. They show us the possibilities of intersectional organising in a French context inimical to intersectional politics. We contend that autonomy in analysis and political action is essential for these movements' survival; autonomy is the condition of possibility for social movements that must seek to counter the violence of political racelessness in France.

In Britain, Sisters Uncut is a minority women-led collective that undertakes actions specifically targeting austerity measures – especially those cuts to anti-violence against women organisations and women's refuges. In the words of one activist:

> 'As a woman of colour I know we have always fought against the double burden of sexist and racist oppression and have always been ignored in our fight. Thirty-two of the domestic violence services that have closed since 2010 were specialist services for BME women … Women are hardest hit by austerity and women of colour harder still. In this context, true representation of our struggle and achievements is non-negotiable.' (The Independent 2015)

This movement is made up of a diverse group of women who, in their "Feministo',[6] describe themselves as 'intersectional feminists' who 'understand that a woman's individual experience of violence is affected by race, class, disability, sexuality and immigration status'. Yet they have one message to those in power, in their stand against austerity and life-threatening cuts to domestic violence services:

> 'Your cuts are sexist, your cuts are dangerous, and you think that you can get away with them because you have

targeted the people who you perceive as powerless. We are those people, we are women, we will not be silenced. We stand united and fight together, and together we will win.' (Sisters Uncut n.d.)

More specifically, they identify the ravages of austerity measures on women, which we discussed in Chapter Three: local councils accepting extremely low bids for public service contracts from organisations that are running anti-violence against women services on shoestring budgets, which are putting the safety of survivors at risk and undermining the working conditions for those who work with survivors.

As in the French examples we have explored, Sisters Uncut illustrate the importance of minority women's activism on their own terms. In Britain, in contrast to France, we have argued that the white Left dominates anti-austerity spaces despite a language of multiculturalism, inclusion and diversity. The white Left's politically raceless rhetoric, which focuses on class and economic inequality at the expense of race, gender and legal status, did not provide political resources or meaningful opportunities for many of our participants. The political practices of Sisters Uncut are all the more powerful and vital for this reason: because their starting point is intersectional, they are able to speak beyond the strictures of white, politically raceless spaces to articulate intersectional critiques of austerity and to undertake creative intersectional mobilisations on their own terms.

Conclusions

In this chapter, we have reflected on our analysis, to learn *across* our three cases, and 'beyond' them.

First, learning across cases means avoiding the straightjacket of 'models' that can obscure similarities as much as it also elucidates differences. When we consider minority women's relations to state power, there are some broad similarities – despite ostensible differences in the interdiction to speak about 'state racism' in France and the chilling effect of the 'gagging bill' in England. Localism does not appear to deliver on its emancipatory promises, as part of the Big Society, and the debate over Scottish independence does not seem to provide progressive alternatives for some of our participants. In these 'difference friendly' cases, minority women's relation to state power does not yield political opportunity, but obstacles and erasure.

Second, 'beyond' is meant in the sense of thinking about the internationalist and autonomous dimensions of intersectional and minority women-led organising that we see in the articulations and actions of new actors and movements such as *Marche de la dignité*, Sisters Uncut and the Mwasi Collectif. When minority women speak and act, on their own terms, they must reach 'beyond' as a condition of political possibility and reject politically raceless movements and politics, where white male voices and bodies dominate, to create their own autonomous political movements and radical new futures and possibilities.

Notes

[1] It also strengthens the legal requirements placed on trade unions in relation to their obligation to keep their list of members up to date.

[2] He was in this role from May 2010 to September 2012.

[3] Given the turmoil following the surprise Brexit vote and the resignation of Prime Minister David Cameron, however, the future of localism and the Big Society are unclear.

[4] Faith-based organisations were not present in our sample, but at the periphery (for example, foodbanks run from churches and mosques). The role of faith in public life is understood quite differently in *laïc* (secular) France – for example a minority woman who advocated unveiling to service users in her organisation – in contrast to England and Scotland. However in all three cases, concerns were raised over how issues such as forced marriage and so-called honour-based violence were instrumentalised, demonising Islam and rendering minority women audible only as victims.

[5] Please visit their website for more information: https://mwasicollectif.com/

[6] Please visit their website for more information: www.sistersuncut.org/feministo/

SEVEN

Conclusion: warning signs

Introduction

In this book, we have examined how minority women survive and resist the French and British austerity regimes. We have demonstrated how the Scottish, English and French contexts create particular opportunities that shape minority women's political behaviour and as well as specific kinds of obstacles. These obstacles often foreclose collective debate and action on minority women's existing intersecting inequalities and austerity's asymmetrical effects. In particular, we have explored how political racelessness operates in each country, despite putative support for multiculturalism and racial equality in Scotland and England, which serves to silence and undermine minority women's social justice claims.

We have also argued that we must resist the temptation to treat minority women's precarity as a fundamentally 'new' experience under austerity. Rather, austerity only worsens an already existing crisis of minority women's economic insecurity. Taking seriously minority women's institutionalised inequality requires a historical understanding of:

- how the European racial contract was constructed as a key organising principle of European modernity;
- how the racial order is sustained in contemporary Europe through racialised policy and practice in which race is never explicitly named;
- how the racial order continues to be defended on both the political Left and Right through a practice of deeming race irrelevant to the European polity.

Further, taking minority women's inequalities seriously also requires a different way of organising and mobilising anti-austerity movements that centre, validate and legitimise minority women as active agents and authors of their lives. Anti-austerity activism necessitates a complex understanding of the dynamics of race, class, gender and legal status. Ignoring race and gender in order to build a falsely unified Left based solely on class and/or populist politics is to wreak profound material and discursive violence on minority women and their interests. Eschewing race and gender also misunderstands how capitalism operates to disproportionately devalue minority women's labour and to depress their income and wealth. Without a working knowledge of racial capitalism, anti-austerity movements will continue to exclude and marginalise minority women for the sake of a mythically all-white, and presumably all-male, working class.

We have also examined how the reshaping of the third sectors in each country dramatically transforms the terms of minority women's activism. As the third sector has been drawn into service delivery that was once performed by the state, and as core funding for third sector organisations has been dramatically cut back, we have seen how some civil society organisations are abandoning their missions to defend and expand the social rights of their constituents in a bid to survive these tough times. In order to gain or maintain their legitimacy – and thus their seat at the table with policy makers – some organisations are transforming themselves to model their private sector counterparts, so that they can better compete for state-based service delivery contracts. As we have demonstrated, this has serious consequences for minority women activists, as their organisations are less likely to be funded in this current austere climate. Minority women's organisations are more likely to be vulnerable to closure as white-led organisations compete for 'market share' of 'niche' social problems related to race, ethnicity and religion. Further, minority women activists who work with and through third sector organisations are likely to have their claims for gender and racial justice refashioned into entrepreneurial actions that individualise inequality and dissipate their radical critiques.

Minority women's DIY activism at the grassroots is, nonetheless, often connected to third sector organisations, and these positive alliances should not be dismissed or ignored. The grassroots politics of survival that we have explored challenges dominant ideas of what constitutes activism and the exclusivity of some variants of social movement theory, which do not name – or worse, which devalue – these spaces. When minority women's DIY activist spaces are misrecognised or erased by white Left activists, and self-care is not understood as political warfare, solidarity cannot be built between activists. We demand that minority women be seen as radical agents, who authorise their own actions, rather than waiting for legitimacy to be conferred upon them by the white Left.

In this final chapter, we consider the current state of European politics and sound the alarm in terms of the mainstreaming of racist and xenophobic political discourse, the erosion of civil liberties and the rise in hate crimes.

Raising the alarm

We have sounded a warning throughout this book about the hegemony of political racelessness and its deleterious impacts on minority women's activism. Political racelessness is not only embedded in the reactionary Right in Europe, but as our empirical analysis has shown, it is also a central organising feature of the European Left. In left-wing spaces that should be sources of solidarity, political racelessness predominates, which silences minority women. As we have argued, a raceless and genderless 'people' and a homogeneous 'working class' can be inimical to the intersectional organising led by minority women. Despite these challenges of political racelessness, we have insisted on the radical critique and activism of minority women and their ongoing politics of survival in a context where they 'cannot afford to be fools of any type', because of Scottish, French and English processes of objectification that deny minority women the 'protections that white skin, maleness and wealth confer' (Hill Collins 2000: 257).

Yet at the time of writing, September 2016, we are forced to sound a further alarm as the European racial contract becomes more explicitly hateful and gains mainstream legitimacy and acceptability, with profound implications for minority women. The prevailing racial order has further hardened, legitimising increasingly racist speech and action. In this new era of 'respectable racism', 'discourses and practices which would qualify as racist according to any reasonable definition of racism … are not perceived as such by the dominant intellectual and political currents' and 'on the contrary, are spread by actors who claim the highest political morality' (Bouamama 2004: 129).

The 'burkini ban' in France

Saïd Bouamama writes of 'respectable racism' in the wake of the 2004 headscarf ban in France. As we see with shocking statements by the French political class to justify the 'burkini ban', this respectability has spread to new spaces – the beach – and to adult women's bodies, whose physical presence at the water's edge is linked seamlessly to the threat of terrorist attacks. The city of Nice banned clothing that 'overtly manifests adherence to a religion at a time when France and places of worship are the target of terrorist attacks', and its mayor wrote in a letter to the French Prime Minister, Manuel Valls, that: 'hiding the face or wearing a full-body costume to go to the beach is not in keeping with our ideal of social relations' (The Guardian 2016a). While the ban was overturned on 1 September 2016, it is the enthusiasm with which the ban was greeted by both political elites and the public that gives us greatest cause for alarm. The 'respectability' of this ban derives from the 'respectable racism' of the state of emergency that followed the attacks on the office of satirical magazine *Charlie Hebdo* and elsewhere in Île-de-France in January 2015. The state of emergency curtailed basic rights and freedoms – of expression, peaceful assembly and association, privacy – despite the condemnation of UN experts, Amnesty and other human rights organisations, who protest the disproportionate and excessive impacts on Muslims in France (United Nations Human Rights Commission 2016).

In order to contain the *Front National*, political parties on both the Right and the Left have reinforced state racism by weaponising *laïcité* [the French understanding of secularism] through the 'securitisation' of everyday life, where some lives are to be 'secured' and defended against the threat of alien Others, who can be stripped of increasingly fragile and precarious protections of citizenship. This racial order has operated long before the 2008 economic crisis, becoming visible in recent memory with the headscarf ban in 2004, and is part of longstanding traditions of repressing Muslim citizens and instrumentalising the bodies of Muslim women, which is directly linked to France's colonial adventures – particularly in Algeria. Now, however, the brazen respectability and acceptability of racism in mainstream discourse is the cause for alarm, as the racial order mutates and comes into plain sight, intervening in new ways on the bodies and in the lives of minority women.

The Brexit vote in the UK

With the surprise June 2016 Brexit vote, new 'respectable racisms' emerged from the shadows in Britain. In the aftermath of the vote, racist attacks spiked. The National Police Chiefs' Council (NPCC) noted that 3,076 hate crimes and incidents were reported to police forces across England, Wales and Northern Ireland between 16 June and 30 June 2016, an increase of 915 reports in comparison to the same period in 2015, and a 42% increase in the reporting of hate crime nationally (NPCC 2016). According to the Institute of Race Relations, there has 'been a return to old school racism, the racism of the '70s and '80s with the most common insults being "Go home"', evidence of which the Institute submitted to the House of Commons

Home Affairs Committee Inquiry into Hate Crime and its Violent Consequences in September 2016 (Institute of Race Relations 2016).

While many policy makers and some sections of the public condemned these racist attacks, it must be noted that these attacks are the legacy of the political classes who helped to undermine public support for multiculturalist policies and who have also organised the hateful, racist and xenophobic 'Leave' campaign that shamelessly echoed the then United Kingdom Independence Party (UKIP) leader Nigel Farage's 'breaking point' politics of migration. The Leave campaigners' promises to stop EU migration and to redirect funds to 'our NHS' were swiftly revoked following the vote to leave the EU. Although the new Conservative government does not seem to know what Brexit means – besides the tautological 'Brexit means Brexit' – migration and xenophobia remain firmly on the agenda in the hands of new Prime Minister Theresa May who, as the former Home Secretary, launched the infamous 'Go home or face arrest' billboard campaign on vans that cruised the streets in English neighbourhoods with large number of minority residents.[1]

The Brexit vote must be read in the broader context of the backlash against multiculturalism, the decline of centre-left parties, the electoral gains of far Right parties and the rise of left-wing and right-wing populism across Europe. Following the Brexit vote, it appears that the British economy is in danger of entering recession and austerity measures are extended into the next decade. The implications of these changes for minority women are unclear, but we must be wary in terms of how they may erase minority women's experiences and reinforce narratives of the privileged, and which reduce the space for the counter-hegemonic actions led by minority women.

We must also relentlessly question what solidarity can mean in the wake of the Brexit vote. Despite documenting institutionalised and everyday racism, minority groups are consistently being ignored and disbelieved. However, in the wake of the xenophobic attacks on 'white' EU migrants fomented by the Brexit campaign, suddenly racism and xenophobia are a public issue requiring political and policy action. Because this 'new racism' appears to be disproportionately affecting 'white' EU migrants, and because this racism has been made visible through the white gaze, racism can now be named and anti-racist action is legitimised (Emejulu 2016). When only what is seen through the white gaze counts and yet, simultaneously, we are told that a focus on race and 'identity politics' weakens the Left and class politics, these empty performances of outrage are exposed as a process of exploiting the emotional labour of people of colour. This is not the path to collective action and it further undermines minority women's intersectional social justice claims (Emejulu 2016).

Silence and complacency in Scotland

In Scotland, the situation is slightly different than in France or England. Unlike France or England, there has been no political entrepreneur who has been able to successfully translate xenophobia and racism into significant electoral gains and political representation in the governing institutions. It must also be remembered that Scotland overwhelmingly voted Remain in the Brexit vote. Although, note, that UKIP does have an elected member of the European Parliament representing Scotland and that fascist graffiti briefly appeared on the streets of Glasgow during the Brexit campaign. Political racelessness plays out in a different way in Scotland – through benign neglect and the hegemony of race-blind universalist politics of Scottish socialism and Scottish nationalism.

Scotland is unique in Europe for its left-wing nationalism that embraces multiculturalism and a seemingly open Scottish national identity. Rather than Scottishness being based on blood or birth, Scottishness is framed as a commitment to a liberal, independent and tolerant Scotland. Because issues of race are not discussed beyond an idea of 'celebrating difference', race, racism and anti-racism are not categories that receive much attention in Scottish public life. It is almost as if the issue of race is settled and can be put aside in order to discuss the more 'important' and 'pressing' issues of Scottish self-determination and independence.

The dominant politics in Scotland create few spaces for debate and action on racism and anti-racism. Thus, we can see how minority women must struggle against a problem of white Scottish ignorance and innocence. Scottish politics are ignorant to everyday and institutionalised racism because class and gender politics supplant any meaningful discussions of racism and anti-racism. Scottish politics also claim innocence because the 'real racism' happens south of the border, in England. In Scotland, political racelessness manifests itself as silence, complacency and smugness about race and racism. Thus, before minority women can make their intersectional claims, they first have to convince their 'allies' and policy makers that there is even a problem to be solved.

Race and Europe: what comes next?

Race is only too present and yet politically absent in European spaces and in the multiple 'crises' in which race disappears. Across Europe, migrants' bodies continue to be weaponised and objectified, as the politics of compassion inevitably give way to restriction and the racial logic of the border prevails.

One year after the death of Alan Kurdi[2], the Syrian boy whose photographed drowned body seemed to briefly open the gates of fortress Europe:

- borders have closed;
- new agreements have been reached (between the EU and Turkey in March 2016, allowing Greece to return 'all new irregular migrants' to Turkey);
- Hungarian right-wing Prime Minister Viktor Orbàn – who has described asylum seekers to Europe as 'a poison' who are not needed or wanted (The Guardian 2016b) – is now a broadly mediatised transnational figure.

Against this backdrop, minority women are, once again, pathologically present but politically absent. They are:

- objectified, as passive wearers of problematic clothing;
- pitied, as refugee women who are victims of the economic crisis but worthy of compassion 'there' and not rights 'here';
- vilified, for failing to prevent their sons and daughters from joining terrorist networks;
- demonised, as part of excessively economically active EU – for which, read 'Polish' – migrant populations undercutting British wages and stealing British jobs.

What politics of survival lie on the horizon? We do not intend to replace existing arrogance and privilege with our own prescriptions of the way forward. Instead, we insist on political attentiveness to the struggles unfolding in new, creative and subversive ways led by minority women at some times and in some places on their own terms.

Note

[1] For detailed empirical analysis, see the 'Mapping Immigration Controversy Project': https://mappingimmigrationcontroversy.com/

[2] For coverage and comments please see: https://www.theguardian.com/world/alan-kurdi

APPENDIX

Fieldwork and sampling strategy

Fieldwork was conducted from September 2011 to May 2014 in the following cities: Glasgow, Edinburgh, (Scotland); London, Manchester, Coventry (England); Paris, Parisian suburbs, Lyon (France). Locating our research in large capitals as well as smaller cities enabled us to compare the experiences of minority women and third sector workers who were located in dense networks (for example London, Paris) with those in areas with smaller, less dense networks (for example Coventry, Glasgow). Participation in, and contact with members of, the Oxfam Routes to Solidarity project event, which focuses on the north of England, also provided further basis for comparison in the fieldwork in England.

Our sample included third sector workers (directors, policy officers and development workers), activist minority women and civil servants (primarily in Scotland) and local government officials with a brief for equalities and/or the third sector. We have selected third sector organisations that are:

- traditional social welfare service providers;
- hybrid organisations combining advocacy and campaigning with service provision;
- organisations offering so-called 'militant provision' – crisis relief and political organising for destitute and/or undocumented migrants;
- campaigning and policy advocacy organisations that are not involved in service provision and are closer to social movements, in that they situate their activity at the edge of social service provision.

While women's organisations and feminist organisations are included in the sample, they were not our focus, as we wanted to explore the extent to which intersectional work – which makes connections between race, gender, legal status and other forms of inequality – was being undertaken by mainstream organisations.

By 'minority women' we refer to women who experience the effects of processes of racialisation, class and gender inequality as well as other sources of inequality, particularly hierarchies of legal status.

We therefore include migrant women in the study. We do not use an essentialist understanding of identity, but one that is process-based and outcome-based. We are therefore also able to encompass the ways in which identity is understood differently across contexts by women themselves (that is, 'difference blind' France, multicultural England).

Our sample includes:

- women who (in the English and Scottish contexts) self-identify as 'Black', a label they use politically;
- women who self-identify as 'refugee' or 'migrant' or who refer to organisations with names including these labels;
- women who, in the course of interviews, refer to their own identity or background, for example 'of immigrant origin' (*d'origine immigrée* in France) or 'my family is from ...'.

The sample also comprises self-identified advocates of specific groups of women, for example asylum seekers and migrants. These advocates were sometimes part of the ethnic majority mainstream – our French sample in particular has a high representation of 'French' advocates – and sometimes self-identified minority women, or women who situated themselves as 'advocates' though also belonging to a minority group they were discussing.

Some participants identified as minority women who, while minoritised along some axes, were advantaged along others, in terms of a higher socioeconomic status through professional employment and higher education qualifications. In some cases, more advantaged minority women specifically identified their status as a resource from which they could draw in order to advocate effectively on behalf of other minority women (for example from their own ethnic group).

In France, we conducted all interviews in French. Interviews were then transcribed in French and translated by us.

Analysis and coding frame

We brought all these data together for the purpose of our analysis. Following transcription, we developed a coding frame that was adapted across all three cases to account for important contextual variation. Considerable time and resources were invested in analysing and fully exploiting the entire corpus. This involved identifying emergent categories and themes, as well as the themes that had been derived deductively, justifying case studies across these 'opposite' contexts.

We organised two Knowledge Exchange and participated in one outreach event:

- '21st Century London Outcasts. Austerity and its Impact on Refugee Families Living in London' organised in collaboration with the Centre for Social Justice and Change and MA in Refugee Studies, University of East London. Activists, academics and third sector workers attended this event on 5 February 2014.
- 'Whose Crisis Counts? Minority Women, Austerity and Solidarity in France and the UK' at the Centre for Education for Racial Equality in Scotland, University of Edinburgh. Participants from the third sector, local and national government and academia attended this workshop on 11 June 2013.
- We were invited Workshop Facilitators and Speakers for 'Routes to Solidarity: Campaigning for Black Women's Rights', organised by Oxfam UK, in Leeds on 26 June 2014.

These events also enhanced data collection and analysis and enabled triangulation. For example, our Knowledge Exchange event in London underscored the significance of the localism agenda for minority women's activism, while participants in the Edinburgh event insisted on the opportunities for 'pro-migrant' political space in Scotland as a form of opposition to Westminster policies.

Details of participants cited in this book are provided in Table A.1.

Table A.2 provides details of participants cited in this book who were part of our sample in our collaborative research (Sosenko et al. 2013) for the Coalition for Racial Equality and Rights, Scotland.

Table A.1 Participants cited

Location	Professional role	Social location/self–identification (and chapter reference)
Lyon	Case worker at migrants' rights centre	French man, Participant FR1, Ch. Four
Edinburgh	Director of an anti-poverty organisation	Woman Note, no further details can be offered as this would reveal her identity, Participant SC1, Ch. Four
London	Director of a migrants' rights organisation	White English man, Participant EN1, Ch. Four
Glasgow	Director of a public health organisation	White Scottish woman, Participant SC2, Ch. Four
London	Development worker in a statutory organisation	Migrant woman, Participant EN2, Ch. Four
Edinburgh	Development worker for a campaigning minority women-led organisation	British Indian woman, Participant SC3, Ch. Four
Paris	Case worker at a militant migrants' rights association	White French woman, Participant FR2, Ch. Four
Glasgow	Policy manager of an anti-poverty organisation	White woman, Participant SC4, Ch.4
Paris	Third sector organisation addressing sex work	French woman, Participant FR3, Ch. Four
London	Head of migrant advocacy organisation	Migrant woman, identifies as non-racialised, Participant, EN3, Ch. Four
Not provided to preserve anonymity	Head of grassroots migrant women initiative	African migrant woman, Participant WA1, Ch. Four
Paris	Marketing worker in a migrant association	French man, Participant FR4, Ch. Four
Edinburgh	Director of a community development organisation	White Scottish man, Participant SC5, Ch. Four
Glasgow	Activist with a DIY minority women's organisation	West African woman, Participant SC6, Ch. Four
Glasgow	Development worker with an anti-poverty organisation	White Scottish woman, Participant SC7, Ch. Four
Glasgow	Activist with a DIY minority women's organisation	West African woman, Participant SC8, Ch. Four

Appendix

Location	Professional role	Social location/self–identification (and chapter reference)
Glasgow	Activist with a DIY minority women's organisation	West African woman, Participant SC9, Ch. Four
London	Director of social enterprise	Refugee woman, Participant EN4, Ch. Four
Manchester	Director of a social enterprise	British Indian woman, Participant EN5, Ch. Four
Coventry	Social entrepreneur and third sector worker	Black woman, Asian woman (identifies as both), Participant EN6, Ch. Four
Paris	Case worker and jurist at a migrants' rights centre	French woman, Participant FR5, Ch. Four
Paris	Housing organisation	French Maghrebi man, Participant FR6, Ch. Four
Paris	Formerly head of an organisation focusing on a specific ethnic group as well as wider public	Minority woman activist, Participant FR7, Ch. Four
Paris	Jurist at migrant advocacy organisation	French man, Participant FR8, Ch. Four
Paris	Housing rights movement	Militant activist woman, Participant FR9, Ch. Four
London	Activist in trade unions and race equality movements	Black activist woman, Participant EN7, Ch. Five
Paris	Head of association working particularly with a specific minority ethnic group as well as wider public	French and specific minority ethnic group identity, Participant FR10, Ch. Five
Paris	Director of militant migrant advocacy organisation	French woman, Participant FR11, Ch. Five
Edinburgh	Development worker for a minority women-led organisation	British Indian woman, Participant SC11, Ch. Five
Glasgow	Focus group with activist women	West African migrant woman, Participant SC12, Ch. Five
Glasgow	Development worker for an anti-poverty organisation	Mixed-race man. Note, no further details can be offered as this would reveal his identity. Participant SC13, Ch. Five
Coventry	Director of women's organisation	British woman, Participant EN8, Ch. Five

Location	Professional role	Social location/self–identification (and chapter reference)
Paris	Director of migrant residence	South American woman, Participant FR12, Ch. Five
Paris	Case worker, militant migrant advocacy organisation	South American woman, Participant FR13, Ch. Five
Manchester	Activist engaged in formal and grassroots political work	British South Asian woman, Participant EN9, Ch. Six
Manchester	Third sector worker	British South Asian man, Participant EN10, Ch. Six
Manchester	Third sector worker	British South Asian woman, Participant EN11, Ch. Six
Glasgow	Development worker for an anti-poverty organisation	Woman. Note, no further details can be offered as this would reveal her identity. Participant SC14, Ch. Six

Table A.2: Coalition for Racial Equality and Rights (CRER) Scotland, participants

Location	Focus group	Social location/self–identification (and chapter reference)
Glasgow	Focus group with Scottish Chinese women	Scottish Chinese woman, CRER Participant 1, Ch. Three
Glasgow	Focus group with Scottish Pakistani women	Scottish Pakistani woman, CRER Participant 2, Ch. Five
Glasgow	Focus group with Scottish Chinese women (quoted in Sosenko et al 2013: 32)	Scottish Chinese woman, CRER Participant 3, Ch. Five
Glasgow	Focus group with Scottish Chinese women	Scottish Chinese woman, CRER Participant 4, Ch. Five

References

Ahmed, S. (2014) 'Selfcare as warfare', *feminist killjoys* blog, 25 August. https://feministkilljoys.com/2014/08/25/selfcare-as-warfare/

Al Ariss, A. and Özbilgin, M. (2010) 'Understanding self-initiated expatriates: Career experiences of Lebanese self-initiated expatriates in France', *Thunderbird International Business Review*, 49, 630-1.

Alcock, P. (2012) *The Big Society: A new policy environment for the third sector?* Working Paper. University of Birmingham. http://www.birmingham.ac.uk/generic/tsrc/documents/tsrc/working-papers/working-paper-82.pdf

Algan, Y., Dustmann, C., Glitz, A. and Manning, A. (2010) 'The economic situation of first and second-generation immigrants in France, Germany and the United Kingdom', *The Economic Journal*, 120, 542, F4-F30.

Algava, É. and Lhommeau, B. (2013) *À l'origine de l'enquête TeO. Enjeux de l'échantillonage, collect et pondérations de l'enquête*. Institut National d'études Démographiques (INED), F1304.

All Party Parliamentary Group on Race and Community (APPG) (2012) *Ethnic minority female unemployment: Black, Pakistani and Bangladeshi heritage women. First report of Session 2012-2013*. London: The Runnymede Trust, 1-27.

Allen, K. and Taylor, Y. (2012a) 'Failed femininities and troubled mothers: Gender and the riots', British Sociological Association, Sociology and the Cuts blog, 17 January.

Allen, K. and Taylor, Y. (2012b) 'Placing parenting, locating unrest: Failed femininities, troubled mothers and riotous subjects', *Studies in the Maternal*, 4, 2. www.mamsie.bbk.ac.uk

Annesley, C. (2012) 'Campaigning against the cuts: Gender equality movements in tough times', *The Political Quarterly*, 83, 1, 19-23.

Baillot, A. and Evain, F. (2012) *Les maternités: Un temps d'accès stable malgré les Fermetures*. Direction de la recherche, des études, de l'évaluation et des statistiques (DREES), 814.

Barkat, S.M. (2005) *Le corps d'exception. Les artifices du pouvoir colonial et la destruction de la vie*. Paris: Editions d'Amsterdam.

Barthélémy, F. (2009) 'Médiateur social, une profession émergente?', *Revue française de sociologie*, 50, 2, 287-314.

Bassel, L. (2012) *Refugee women: Beyond gender versus culture*. London: Routledge.

Bassel, L. (2014) 'Contemporary grammars of resistance: Two French social movements', *Sociology*, 48, 3, 537-53.

Bassel, L. (forthcoming) *The politics of listening: Possibilities and challenges for democratic life*. London: Palgrave.

Bassel, L. and Emejulu, A. (2010) 'Struggles for institutional space in France and the UK: Intersectionality and the politics of policy', *Politics and Gender*, 6, 4, 517-44.

Bassel, L. and Emejulu, A. (2014) 'Solidarity under austerity: Intersectionality in France and the United Kingdom', *Politics and Gender*, 10, 1, 130-6.

Bassel, L. and Emejulu, A. (forthcoming) 'Caring subjects: Migrant women and the third sector in England and Scotland', in U. Erel and T. Reynolds (guest eds) *Ethnic and Racial Studies*. Special issue on 'Migrant Mothers Challenging Racialized Citizenship'.

Bassel, L. and Lloyd, C. (2011) 'Rupture or reproduction? "New" citizenship in France', *French Politics*, 9, 1, 21-49.

Beatty, C. and Fothergill, S. (2013) *Hitting the poorest places hardest. The local and regional impact of welfare reform*. Sheffield Hallam University, Scottish Parliament, Financial Times.

Bentchicou, N. (ed.) (1997) *Les femmes de l'immigration au quotidien*. Paris: Licorne/l'Harmattan.

Bertossi, C., Duyvendak, J.W. and Scholten, P. (2015) 'The coproduction of national models of integration: A view from France and the Netherlands', in P. Scholten, H. Entzinger, R. Penninx and S. Verbeek (eds) *Integrating immigrants in Europe: Research-policy dialogues* (IMISCOE research series). Cham: Springer, 59-76.

Bhambra, G.K. (2016) 'Whither Europe? Postcolonial versus neocolonial cosmopolitanism', *Interventions*, 18, 2, 187-202.

Bock, G. and James, S. (1992) (eds) *Beyond equality and difference*. London: Routledge.

Bouadbillah, P. (1997) 'Les femmes relais et leur action', in N. Bentchicou (ed.) *Les femmes de l'immigration au quotidien*. Paris: Licorne/L'Harmattan, 72-7.

Bouamama, S. (1994) *Dix ans de marche des Beurs:Chronique d'un mouvement avorté*. Paris: Desclée de Brouwer.

Bouamama, S. (2004) *L'affaire du foulard islamique. La production d'un racisme respectable*. Roubaix: Geai Bleu.

Bouamama, S. and Femmes du Blanc-Mesnil [Women of Blanc-Mesnil] (2013) *Femmes des quartiers populaires. En résistance contre les discriminations* [Women from the popular neighbourhoods/quarters. In resistance against discriminations]. Paris: Le Temps des Cerises.

Bouteldja, H. (2004) 'De la cérémonie du dévoilement à Alger (1958) à Ni Putes Ni Soumises: l'instrumentalisation coloniale et néo-coloniale de la cause des femmes'. http://lmsi.net/De-la-ceremonie-du-devoilement-a

Bowen, J.R. (2007) *Why the French don't like headscarves: Islam, the state, and public space*. Princeton: Princeton University Press.

Boyer, R. (2012) 'The four fallacies of contemporary austerity policies: The lost Keynesian legacy', *Cambridge Journal of Economics*, 36, 1, 283-312.

Brewer, M. and Browne, J. (2011) 'Cuts to welfare spending', in Yeates, N., Haux, T., Jawad, R. and Kilkey, M. (eds) *In defence of welfare. The impact of the spending review*. Lavenham: Social Policy Association.

Brinbaum, Y. and Guégnard, C. (2012) 'Parcours de formation et d'insertion des jeunes issus de l'immigration au prisme de l'orientation', *Formation emploi*, 118.

Brinbaum, Y. and Kieffer, A. (2009) 'Les scolarités des enfants d'immigrés de la sixième au baccalauréat: Différenciation et polarisation des parcours', *Population*, 64, 3, 561-610.

Bunel, M., L'Horty, Y. and Petit, P. (2016) 'Les discriminations a l'embauche dans la sphere publique: Effects respectifs de l'address et de l'origine', *Travail, Employ et Politiques Publiques*. http://www.tepp.eu/doc/users/268/bib/desperadopdf_9239.pdf

Butler, V. (2012) *Ethnic minority female unemployment: Black, Pakistani and Bangladeshi heritage women*, London: All Party Parliamentary Group.

Canet, R., Pech, L. and Stewart, M. (2015) 'France's burning issue: Understanding the urban riots of November 2005', in M.T. Davis (ed.) *Crowd actions in Britain and France from the Middle Ages to the Modern World*. London: Palgrave Macmillan UK, 270-92.

Canovan, M. (1999) 'Trust the people! Populism and the two faces of democracy', *Political Studies*, 47, 1, 2-16.

Carmel, E. and Harlock, J. (2008) 'Instituting the "third sector" as a governable terrain: Partnership, procurement and performance in the UK', *Policy & Politics*, 36, 2, 155-71.

CEMVO (Council for Ethnic Minority Voluntary Organisations) (2010) *The impact of the economic downturn on BME VCOs*. London: CEMVO.

Chanial, P. and Laville, J.L. (2004) 'French civil society experiences: Attempts to bridge the gap between political and economic dimensions', in A. Evers and J.L. Laville (eds) *The third sector in Europe*. Cheltenham: Edward Elgar Publishing.

Cheutin, F.D.R. (2016) 'Sarkozy fier de ses propos sur "la racaille"', *La Provence,* June.

Choudry, A. and Kapoor, D. (eds) (2013) *NGOization: Complicity, contradictions and prospects.* London: Zed.

Choudry, A. and Shragge, E. (2011) 'Disciplining dissent: NGOs and community organizations', *Globalizations*, 8, 4, 503-17.

Chrisafis, A. (2011) 'France's burqa ban: Women are "effectively under house arrest"', *The Guardian*, 19 September.

Clarke, J. and Newman, J. (1997) *The managerial state: Power, politics and ideology in the remaking of social welfare.* London: Sage.

Clarke, J. and Newman, J. (2012) 'The alchemy of austerity', *Critical Social Policy*, 32, 3, 299-319.

Cohen-Emerique, M. (1993) 'La médiation assurée par les femmes relais', *Accueillir*, 193, 13.

Collombet, C. and Hiltunen, A. (2013) 'Les systèmes de protection sociale européens face à la crise: Entre ajustements paramétriques et mutations structurelles', *Informations sociales*, 6, 180, 72-81.

Colombo, E. (2015) 'Multiculturalisms: An overview of multicultural debates in Western societies', *Current Sociology*, 800-824.

Commission on the Future Delivery of Public Services (Christie Commission) (2011) *Commission on the Future Delivery of Public Services Final Report.* www.gov.scot/resource/doc/352649/0118638.pdf

Communities and Local Government (2011) *A plain English guide to the Localism Act.* London: Department for Communities and Local Government. https://www.gov.uk/government/uploads/system/uploads/attachment_data/file/5959/1896534.pdf

Connolly, W. (1991) *Identity/difference: Democratic negotiations of political paradox.* Ithaca: Cornell University Press.

Cours des comptes (2012) *Analyses de l'execution du budget de l'État par missions et programmes.* Paris: Cours des comptes.

Crawford, C. and Greaves, E. (2015) *Socio-economic, ethnic and gender differences in HE participation*, Institute for Fiscal Studies, 186.

Delcroix, C. (1995) *Rôles et perspectives des femmes relais en France.* Paris: Agence pour le développement des relations interculturelles (ADRI).

Delcroix, C. (1997) 'Médiatrices socioculturelles, citoyennes innovantes!', in N. Bentchicou (ed.) *Les femmes de l'immigration au quotidien.* Paris: Licorne/L'Harmattan, 41-54.

Délégation interministérielle à la ville (2004) Rapport de l'Observatoire des ZUS. http://www.ville.gouv.fr/IMG/pdf/observatoire-rapport-2004_cle216a4c.pdf

Delphy, C. (2005) *Race, caste et genre en France.* http://lmsi.net/Race-caste-et-genre-en-France

Delphy, C. (2015a) *Separate and dominate: Feminism and racism after the War on Terror.* London: Verso Books.

Delphy, C. (2015b) *La religion, une affaire privée? Réfutation d'une idée reçue*, LMSI.net. http://lmsi.net/La-religion-une-affaire-privee

Diani, M. (1992) 'The concept of a social movement', *The Sociological Review*, 40, 10, 1-25.

Dikeç, M. (2007) 'Revolting geographies: Urban unrest in France', *Geography Compass*, 1, 5, 1190-206.

Diochon, M. and Anderson, A.R. (2011) 'Ambivalence and ambiguity in social enterprise: Narratives and values in reconciling purpose and practices', *International Entrepreneurship and Management Journal*, 7, 1, 93-109.

Dominelli, L. (2006) *Women and community action*. Bristol: Policy Press.

Dremeaux, L. (2016) 'For Muslim women, a daily "struggle"; Even after growing up in Europe, many feel shunned and alienated', *International New York Times*, 3 September.

Dugué, E. and Rist, B. (2002) 'Des femmes-relais aux médiatrices socio-culturelles: Des compétences reconnues, un métier en débat', *Recherche sociale*, 163, 32-41.

Duhamel, E. and H. Joyeux (2013) 'Femmes et précarité. Étude du Conseil économique, social et environnemental, Délégation aux droits des femmes et à l'égalité', *Journal Officiel de la République française*, 2013-09 NOR: CESL1100009X.

Economist, The (2013) 'Must We Work Harder?', *The Economist*, 22 June. http://www.economist.com/news/europe/21579827-socialist-president-who-has-no-alternative-cut-pension-and-welfare-spending-faces

Emejulu, A (2008) 'The intersection of ethnicity, poverty and wealth', in T. Ridge and S. Wright (eds) *Understanding inequality, poverty and wealth*. Bristol: Policy Press, 155-80.

Emejulu, A. (2011) 'Can "the people" be feminists? Analysing the fate of feminist justice claims in populist grassroots movements in the United States', *Interface: Special Issue on Feminism, Women's Movements and Women in Movements*, 3, 2, 123-51.

Emejulu, A. (2013) 'Being and belonging in Scotland: Exploring the intersection of ethnicity, gender and national identity among Scottish Pakistani groups', *Scottish Affairs*, 84, 3, 41-64.

Emejulu, A. (2015) *Community development as micropolitics: Comparing theories, policies and politics in America and Britain*. Bristol: Policy Press.

Emejulu, A. (2016) 'On the hideous whiteness of Brexit'. Verso Books. www.versobooks.com/blogs/2733-on-the-hideous-whiteness-of-brexit-let-us-be-honest-about-our-past-and-our-present-if-we-truly-seek-to-dismantle-white-supremacy

Emejulu, A. and Bassel, L. (2013) *Between Scylla and Charybdis: Enterprise and austerity as a double hazard for non-governmental organisations in France and the UK*, Centre for Education for Racial Equality in Scotland, Briefing No. 2. www.ceres.education.ed.ac.uk/wp-content/uploads/Briefing-No.2.pdf

Emejulu, A. and Bassel, L. (2015) 'Minority women, activism and austerity', *Race & Class*, 57, 2, 86-95.

Esping-Andersen, G. (1990) *The three worlds of welfare capitalism.* Princeton: Princeton University Press.

Esping-Andersen, G. (1999) *Social foundations of postindustrial economies.* Oxford: Oxford University Press.

European Women's Lobby (2016) 'Violence against women in Cologne: Statement Deutscher Frauenrat'. www.womenlobby.org/Violence-against-women-in-Cologne-statement-Deutscher-Frauenrat-on

Eydoux, A. (2014) 'Women during recessions in France and Germany. The gender biases of public policies', *Revue de L'OFCE - Débats et Politiques*, 133, 2, 153-88.

Fassin, É. (2015) '(Sexual) whiteness and national identity', in K. Murji and J. Solomos (eds) *Theories of race and ethnicity. Contemporary debates and perspectives.* Cambridge: Cambridge University Press, 233-50.

Faure, S. and Vécrin, A. (2015) 'Le débat sans fin des statistiques ethniques', *Libération*, 4 February

Felouzis, G. (2003) 'La ségrégation ethnique au collège et ses conséquences', *Revue française de sociologie*, 44, 413-47.

Fernando, M.L. (2013) 'Save the Muslim woman, save the Republic: Ni Putes Ni Soumises and the ruse of neoliberal sovereignty', *Modern & Contemporary France*, 21, 2.

Forum de la performance (2012) *La révision générale des politiques publiques.* http://www.performance-publique.budget.gouv.fr/performance-gestion-publiques/archives-modernisation-etat-demarches-anterieures/essentiel/revision-generale-politiques-publiques/revision-generale-politiques-publiques#.WLlsuhicYlU

Freedman, J. (2007) 'Droit d'asile pour les femmes persécutées? La Convention de Genève revisitée', in J. Freedman and J. Valluy (eds) *Persécutions des femmes. Savoirs, mobilisations et protections.* Broissieux: Editions du Croquant, 451-508.

Freeman, G. (2004) 'Immigrant incorporation in Western democracies', *International Migration Review*, 38, 3, 945-69.

Fricker, M. (2008) 'Forum on Miranda Fricker's "Epistemic Injustice: Power and the Ethics of Knowing"', *Theoria*, 23, 1, 69-71.

Frickey, A. and Primon, J.-L. (2006) 'Une double pénalisation pour les non-diplomées du supérieur d'origine nord-africaine?', *Formation emploi*, 94, 27-43.

Gitlin, T. (1995) *The twilight of common dreams: Why America is wracked by culture wars*. New York: Metropolitan Books.

Gobillon, L., Rupert, P. and Wasmer, E. (2014) 'Ethnic unemployment rates and frictional markets', *Journal of Urban Economics*, 79, 108-20.

Goldberg, D.T. (2006) 'Racial Europeanization', *Ethnic and Racial Studies*, 29, 2, 331-64.

Guardian, The (2005) 'Integration has to be voluntary', Leader, 5 November. https://www.theguardian.com/news/2005/nov/06/leaders.france

Guardian, The (2014) 'Lobbying Bill passes House of Lords', 28 January. www.theguardian.com/politics/2014/jan/28/lobbying-bill-passes-house-lords

Guardian, The (2016a) 'Nice becomes latest French city to impose burkini ban', 19 August. https://www.theguardian.com/world/2016/aug/19/nice-becomes-latest-french-city-to-impose-burkini-ban

Guardian, The (2016b) 'Hungarian prime minister says migrants are 'poison' and 'not needed'', 26 July. https://www.theguardian.com/world/2016/jul/26/hungarian-prime-minister-viktor-orban-praises-donald-trump

Hancock, A.-M. (2004) *The politics of disgust: The public identity of the Welfare Queen*. New York: New York University Press.

Hastings, A., Bailey, N., Bramley, G., Gannon, M. and Watkins, D. (2015) *The cost of the cuts: The impact on local government and poorer communities*. York: Joseph Rowntree Foundation.

Hesse, B. (2007) 'Racialized modernity: An analytics of white mythologies', *Ethnic and Racial Studies*, 30, 4, 643-63.

Hill Collins, P. (2000) *Black feminist thought: Knowledge, consciousness and the politics of empowerment*. New York: Routledge.

Hirsch, D. (2015) *A minimum income standard for the UK in 2015*. Joseph Rowntree Foundation.

Hobsbawm, E. (1996) 'Identity politics and the Left', *New Left Review*, 217, 38-45.

iAGS (Independent Annual Growth Survey) (2014) *From austerity to stagnation. How to avoid the deflation trap. The independent annual growth survey*. Paris: Organisation Française de conjonctures Economiques (French Economic Research Observatory), Economic Council of the Labour Movement, Insitut für Makroökonomie und Konjunkturforschung (Macroeconomic Policy Institute).

Imkaan (2015) *State of the sector: Contextualising the current experiences of BME ending violence against women and girls organisations*. http://www.endviolenceagainstwomen.org.uk/data/files/resources/74/IMKAAN-STATE-OF-THE-SECTOR-FINAL.pdf

Independent, The (2015) 'Why I protested with Sisters Uncut at the Suffragette premiere', 8 October. www.independent.co.uk/voices/why-i-protested-with-sisters-uncut-at-the-premiere-of-suffragette-a6685686.html

Indigènes de la République (2005) '"Nous sommes les indigènes de la République!" Appel pour des Assises de l'anti-colonialisme post-colonial'. http://lmsi.net/Nous-sommes-les-indigenes-de-la

Indigènes de la République (2010) 'Political principles of the Parti des Indigènes de la République'. www.decolonialtranslation.com/english/pirfoundingdocEng.html#_edn- ref1

Insee (Insitut National de la statistique et des études économiques) (2015) *Évolution du PIB en France jusqu'en 2015*. www.insee.fr/fr/themes/tableau.asp?reg_id=0&id=159%3E

Institute of Race Relations (2016) 'Submission to the House of Commons Home Affairs Committee on Hate Crime and its Violent Consequences.' 1 September. www.irr.org.uk/news/submission-to-the-house-of-commons-home-affairs-committee-on-hate-crime-and-its-violent-consequences/

Ireland, D. (2005) 'Why is France burning? The rebellion of a lost generation', *Direland* weblog. http://direland.typepad.com/direland/2005/11/why_is_france_b.html

Jacobs, K. and T. Manzi (2013) 'New localism, old retrenchment: The "Big Society", housing policy and the politics of welfare reform', *Housing, Theory and Society*, 30, 1, 29-45.

Jérôme, B. (2011) 'Le non-remplacement d'un fonctionnaire sur deux a atteint ses limites, selon un rapport parlementaire', *Le Monde*, 12 October.

Jones, O. (2011) *Chavs: The demonization of the working class*. London: Verso.

Joppke, C. (2004) 'The retreat of multiculturalism in the liberal state: Theory and policy', *The British Journal of Sociology*, 55, 2, 237-57.

Joppke, C. (2007a) 'Beyond national models: Civic integration policies for immigrants in Western Europe', *West European Politics*, 30, 1, 1-22.

Joppke, C. (2007b) 'Transformation of immigrant integration: Civic integration and antidiscrimination in the Netherlands, France, and Germany', *World Politics*, 59, 2, 243–73.

Kamat, S. (2004) 'The privatization of public interest: Theorizing NGO discourse in a neoliberal era', *Review of International Political Economy*, 11, 1, 155-76.

Kamenou, N., Netto, G. and Fearfull, A. (2013) 'Ethnic minority women in the Scottish labour market: Employers' perceptions', *British Journal of Management*, 24, 398-413.

Kenway, P. and Palmer, G. (2007) *Poverty among ethnic groups: How and why does it differ?* York: Joseph Rowntree Foundation.

Kymlicka, W. (2010) 'The rise and fall of multiculturalism? New debates on inclusion and accommodation in diverse societies', *International Social Science Journal*, 61, 199, 97-112.

L'Horty, Y. and Sari, F. (2008) *Les zones urbaines sensibles en Ile-de-France: Typologie des tensions territoriales*. http://www.cee-recherche.fr/publications/document-de-travail/les-zones-urbaines-sensibles-en-ile-de-france-typologie-des-tensions-territoriales

L'Obs (2016) '"Musulman Discret": "Non je prie pas. Je vérifie juste la platitude du Tapis"', *Le Nouvel Observateur*, 18 August.

Laclau, E. (2005) *On populist reason*. London: Verso.

Lafarge, F. and Le Clainche, M. (2010) 'La révision générale des politiques publiques', *Revue française d'administration publique*, 136, 751-4.

Lannelongue, M.-P. (2015) 'L'édito', *M, le magazine du Monde*, 24 October.

Le Cour Grandmaison, O. (2010) *De l'indigénat. Anatomie d'un 'monstre' juridique: le droit colonial en Algérie et dans l'empire français*. Paris: La Découverte/Zones.

Le Monde (2006) 'A Aulnay-sous-Bois, le travail de fourmi des "femmes relais" pour leur quartier', 23 October.

Le Monde (2015) 'Une Marche de la dignité à Paris contre les violences policières', 31 October. www.lemonde.fr/societe/article/2015/10/31/une-marche-de-la-dignite-a-paris-contre-les-violences-policieres_4800681_3224.html#HZ8U7D1raYjCTTbu.99

Libération (2008) 'Assurance chômage: ce qui va changer en 2009', 24 December.

Lloyd, C. (1995) 'International comparisons in the field of ethnic relations', in A.G. Hargreaves and J. Leaman (eds) *Racism, ethnicity and politics in contemporary Europe*. Aldershot: Elgar.

Lombardo, P. and Pujol, J. (2010) *Niveau de vie et pauvreté des immigrés en 2007*. Paris: Insee.

Lombardo, P. and Pujol, J. (2011) *Le niveau de vie des descendants d'immigrés*. Paris: Insee.

Lonergan, G. (2015) 'Migrant women and social reproduction under austerity', *Feminist Review*, 109.

Lorde, A. (1984) *Sister outsider: Essays and speeches.* New York: Ten Speed Press.

Lorde, A. (1988) *A burst of light.* New York: Firebrand Books.

Lugones, M. (2010) 'Toward a decolonial feminism', *Hypatia*, 25, 4, 742-59.

MacDonald, R., Shildrick, T.A. and Furlong, A. (2013) 'In search of "intergenerational cultures of worklessness": Hunting the Yeti and shooting Zombies', *Critical Social Policy,* 34, 2, 199-220.

Macmillan, R., Taylor, R., Arvidson, M., Soteri-Proctor, A. and Teasdale, S. (2013) *The third sector in unsettled times: A field guide.* Working Paper. University of Birmingham. http://www.birmingham.ac.uk/generic/tsrc/documents/tsrc/working-papers/working-paper-109.pdf

Maiguashca, B., Dean, J.M. and Keith, D. (2016) 'Pulling together in a crisis? Anarchism, feminism and the limits of left-wing convergence in austerity Britain', *Capital and Class*, 40, 1, 37-57.

Marchal, S., Marx, I. and Van Mechelen, N. (2014) 'The great wake-up call? Social citizenship and minimum income provisions in Europe in times of crisis', *Journal of Social Policy*, 43, 2, 247-67.

Martens, K. (2002) 'Mission impossible? Defining nongovernmental organisations', *Voluntas: International Journal of Voluntary and Nonprofit Organisations*, 13, 3, 271-85.

Marty, C. (2011) 'Impact de la crise et de l'austérité sur les femmes: des raisons de s'indigner et se mobiliser', *Le Blog d'Attac*, weblog. https://blogs.attac.org/commission-genre/article/impact-de-la-crise-et-de-l

Marty, C. (2012) 'Les femmes face à la crise et à l'austérité', *Crise et alternatives en Europe*, 172-9 http://www.espaces-marx.net/IMG/pdf/T_N10_Marty.pdf

Marty, C. (2015) 'Les françaises ne sont pas épargnées', *Le Blog d'Attac* weblog. https://blogs.attac.org/IMG/pdf/tgs_controverse_austerite_cmarty.pdf

Maxwell, R. (2010) 'Political participation in France among non-European-origin migrants: Segregation or integration?', *Journal of Ethnic and Migration Studies*, 36, 3, 425-43.

Mayblin, L. and Soteri-Proctor, A. (2011) *The Black Minority Ethnic third sector: A resource paper*, TSRC Working Paper 58. Birmingham: Third Sector Research Centre.

McCormick, J. and Philo, C. (1995) 'Where is poverty? The hidden geography of poverty in the United Kingdom', in C. Philo (ed.) *Off the map: The social geography of poverty in the UK.* London: Child Poverty Action Group, 1–22.

McCrone, D. and Bechhofer, F. (2008) 'National identity and social inclusion', *Ethnic and Racial Studies*, 31, 7, 1245-66.

Mendoza, M. (1997) 'Le point sur les femmes-relais', *La lettre de la DPM*, 39 (octobre).

Merckling, O. (2002) 'L'emploi des femmes étrangères et issues de l'immigration', *Hommes et Migrations*, 1239, 100-11.

Métral, A. (2016) *Genre et crise économique: Un impact inégalitaire.* Pour la Solidarité.

Meurs, D. and Pailhé, A. (2008) 'Descendantes d'immigrés en France: Une double vulnérabilité sur le marché du travail?', *Travail, Genre et Sociétés*, 20, 87-107.

Meurs, D. and Pailhé, A. (2010) 'Position sur le marché du travail des descendants directs d'immigrés en France: les femmes doublement désavantagées ?', *Économie et Statistique,* 431(1), 129-151.

Milbourne, L. (2013) *Voluntary sector in transition.* Bristol: Policy Press.

Milbourne, L. and Cushman, M. (2013) 'From the third sector to the Big Society: How changing UK government policies have eroded third sector trust', *VOLUNTAS: International Journal of Voluntary and Nonprofit Organizations*, 24, 2, 485-508.

Mills, C.W. (1997) *The racial contract.* Ithaca: Cornell University Press.

Mills, C.W. (2007) 'White ignorance', in S. Sullivan and N. Tuana (eds) *Race and epistemologies of ignorance.* Albany: SUNY Press.

Minces, J. (2006) 'Un accélérateur de l'émancipation des femmes', *Hommes & Migrations*, 1259, 84-6.

Minni, C. and Okba, M. (2014) *Emploi et chômage des descendants d'immigrés en 2012.* Ministère du Travail, de l'Emploi, de la Formation professionnelle et du Dialogue social. http://travail-emploi.gouv.fr/IMG/pdf/2014-023.pdf

Mirza, H.S. (1997) *Black British feminism: A reader.* London: Routledge.

Mirza, H.S. (2015) 'Harvesting our collective intelligence: Black British feminism in post-race times', *Women's Studies International Forum*, 51, 1-9.

Modood, T. (2013) *Multiculturalism.* London: Polity.

Moore, J. (2016) 'Why the New Year's attacks on women in Germany weren't even a crime', 26 March. https://www.buzzfeed.com/jinamoore/cologne-attacks-on-women?utm_term=.qkRa17Mkm#.wc1q7Y8LR

Mwasi Collectif (n.d.) Qui Nous Sommes. https://mwasicollectif.com

National Police Chiefs' Council (NPCC) (2016) 'Hate crime undermines the diversity and tolerance we should instead be celebrating.' 8 July. http://news.npcc.police.uk/releases/hate-crime-undermines-the-diversity-and-tolerance-we-should-instead-be-celebrating-1

Netto, G., Hudson, M., Noon, M., Sosenko, F., De Lima, P. and Kamenou, N. (2015) 'Migration, ethnicity and progression from low-paid work: Implications for skills policy', *Social Policy & Society*, 14, 4, 509-22.

Neville, S. (2016) 'Cuts to hit Asian communities hard as big families bear brunt of reforms', *Financial Times*, 9 March.

Newman, J. (2013) 'Spaces of power: Feminism, neoliberalism and gendered labor', *Social Politics*, 20, 2, 200-21.

Nicholls, W.J. (2006) 'Associationalism from above: Explaining failure through France's Politique de la Ville', *Urban Studies*, 43, 10, 1779-802.

Ni Putes Ni Soumises (2005) [Website grey literature on file with authors]. www.npns.fr/l-association-ni-putes-ni-soumises/presentation/

OECD (Organisation for Economic Co-operation and Development) (2008) *OECD employment outlook 2008*. Paris: OECD.

OECD (2010) 'Migration and Unemployment', in *OECD Factbook 2010: Economic, Environmental and Social Statistics*. Paris: OECD Publishing. DOI: http://dx.doi.org/10.1787/factbook-2010-8-en

OECD (2012) *Economic policy reforms 2012: Going for growth*. Paris: OECD Publishing.

OECD (2014) *Panorama de la société 2014: Les indicateurs sociaux de l'OCDE*. Paris: OECD Publishing.

Office for National Statistics (2012) *Ethnicity and national identity in England and Wales 2011*, 1-14. https://www.ons.gov.uk/peoplepopulationandcommunity/culturalidentity/ethnicity/articles/ethnicityandnationalidentityinenglandandwales/2012-12-11

Okba, M. (2009) *Habiter en Zus et être immigré: Un double risque sur le marché du travail*, 48.1, Dares. http://dares.travail-emploi.gouv.fr/IMG/pdf/2009-11-48-1.pdf

Pan Ké Shon, J.-L. (2009) 'Ségrégation ethnique et ségrégation sociale en quartiers sensibles. L'apport des mobilités résidentielles', *Revue française de sociologie*, 50, 3, 451-87.

Patacchini, E. and Zenou, Y. (2005) 'Spatial mismatch, transport mode and search decisions in England', *Journal of Urban Economics*, 58, 62-90.

Pereira, I. (2010) *Les grammaires de la contestation. Un guide de la gauche radicale*. Paris: La Découverte.

Périvier, H. (2014) 'Men and women during the economic crisis. Employment trends in eight European countries', *Revue de L'OFCE – Débats et Politiques*, 133, 2, 41-84.

Périvier, H. and Silvera, R. (2015) 'Au nom de l'austérité?', *Travail, Genre et Sociétés*, 33, 1, 123-6.

Phillips, T. (2005) *Sleepwalking to segregation?* https://www.jiscmail.ac.uk/cgi-bin/webadmin?A3=ind0509&L=CRONEM&E=quoted-printable&P=60513&B=-------_%3D_NextPart_001_01C5C28A.09501783&T=text%2Fhtml;%20charset=iso-8859-1&pending=

Phoenix, A. (1987) 'Theories of gender and black families', in G. Weiner and M. Arnot (eds) *Gender under scrutiny*. London: Hutchinson, 50-63.

Phoenix, A. and Phoenix, A. (2012) 'Racialisation, relationality and riots: Intersections and interpellations', *Feminist Review*, 100, 52-71.

Platt, L. (2007) *Poverty and Ethnicity in the UK*. York: Joseph Rowntree Foundation.

Poinsot, M. (2001) 'Le mouvement associatif, un instrument au service des politiques publiques d'intégration', *Hommes et Migrations*, 1229, 64-75.

Pulham, S. (2005) 'How the "rabble" gave Sarkozy a lesson on the power of language', *The Guardian*, 11 November.

Quiminal, C. (1997) 'Un reseau d'associations de femmes africaines', *Hommes et Migrations*, 1208.

Quiminal, C., Diouf, B., Fall, B., and Timera, M. (1995) *Mobilisation associative et dynamiques d'intégration des femmes d'Afrique subsaharienne en France*. Paris: Ministère des Affaires Sociales, de la Santé et de la Ville, Direction de la Population et des Migrations.

Robinson, C.J. (1983) *Black Marxism: The making of the Black radical tradition*. Chapel Hill: University of North Carolina Press

ROTA (Race on the Agenda) (2009) *The economic downturn and the Black, Asian and minority ethnic Third Sector*. London: ROTA.

Rowbotham, S., Segal, L. and Wainwright, H. (eds) (1979) *Beyond the fragments: Feminism and the making of socialism*. London: Newcastle Socialist Centre and Islington Community Press.

Sabbagh, D. and Peer, S. (2008) 'French colour blindness in perspective. The controversy over "statistiques ethniques"', *French Politics, Culture & Society*, 26, 1, 1-6.

Sandhu, K., Stephenson, M.-A. and Harrison, J. (2013) *Layers of inequality: A human rights and equality impact assessment of the public spending cuts on BAME women in Coventry.* Coventry: Coventry Women's Voices, Coventry Ethnic Minority Action Partnership, Foleshill Women's Training and the Centre for Human Rights in Practice, School of Law, University of Warwick.

Scotland's Census (2013) *Release 2A – 26 September.* www.scotlandscensus.gov.uk/en/censusresults/bulletinr2.html

Scottish Government (2015) A Stronger Scotland: The Government Programme for Scotland 2015-2016. http://www.gov.scot/Resource/0048/00484439.pdf

Seguino, S. (2010) 'The global economic crisis, its gender and ethnic implications, and policy responses', *Gender & Development*, 18, 2, 179-99.

Shabi, R. (2016) 'Burkini ban: New wave of French "mission civilisatrice"', *Al Jazeera International*, 28 August. www.aljazeera.com/indepth/opinion/2016/08/burkini-ban-wave-french-mission-civilatrice-160828110929500.html%3E

Simon, P. (2007) *Statistiques 'ethniques' et protection des données dans les pays du Conseil de l'Europe.* Strasbourg: Conseil de l'Europe.

Simon, P. (2008a) 'Les statistiques, les sciences sociales françaises et les rapports sociaux ethniques et de "race"', *Revue française de Sociologie*, 49, 153-62.

Simon, P. (2008b) 'The choice of ignorance: The debate on ethnic and racial statistics in France', *French Politics, Culture and Society*, 26, 1, 7-31.

Simon, P. (2010) 'Statistics, French social sciences and ethnic and racial social relations', *Revue française de Sociologie*, 51, 159.

Simon, P. (2012) 'Collecting ethnic statistics in Europe: A review', *Ethnic and Racial Studies*, 35, 1366-91.

Sintomer, Y. and De Maillard, J. (2007) 'The limits to local participation and deliberation in the French "politique de la ville"', *European Journal of Political Research*, 46, 4, 503-29.

Sisters Uncut (n.d.) Feministo. http://www.sistersuncut.org/feministo

Smith, M. and Villa, P. (2014) 'The long tail of the Great Recession: Foregone employment and foregone policies', *Revue de L'OFCE - Débats et Politiques*, 133, 2, 85-119.

Sommerlad, H. and Sanderson, P.J. (2013) 'Social justice on the margins: The future of the not for profit sector as providers of legal advice in England and Wales', *Journal of Social Welfare and Family Law*, 35, 2.

Sosenko, F., Netto, G., Emejulu, A. and Bassel, L. (2013) *In it together? Perceptions on ethnicity, recession and austerity in three Glasgow communities.* Glasgow: Coalition for Racial Equality and Rights. www.crer.org.uk/Publications/inittogether.pdf

Standing, G. (2011) *The Precariat: The new dangerous class.* London: Bloomsbury.

Strolovitch, D.Z. (2007) *Affirmative advocacy. Race, class and gender in interest group politics.* Chicago: University of Chicago Press.

Strolovitch, D.Z. (2013) 'Of Mancessions and Hecoveries: Race, gender, and the political construction of economic crises and recoveries', *Perspectives on Politics*, 11, 1, 167-76.

Sudbury, J. (1998) *Other kinds of dreams: Black women's organisations and the politics of transformation.* London: Routledge.

Taylor, M. (2015) '"Vast social cleansing" pushes tens of thousands of families out of London', *The Guardian*, 28 August.

Taylor-Gooby, P. (2011) 'Root and branch restructuring to achieve major cuts: The social policy programme of the 2010 UK Coalition government', *Social Policy and Administration*, 46, 1, 1-22.

Taylor-Gooby, P. (2013) *The double crisis of the welfare state and what we can do about it.* Basingstoke: Palgrave Macmillan UK.

Taylor-Gooby, P. and Stoeker, G. (2010) 'The Coalition programme: A new vision for Britain or politics as usual?', *The Political Quarterly*, 82, 1, 4-15.

Theodoropoulou S. and Watt, A. (2011) *Withdrawal symptoms: An assessment of the austerity packages in Europe.* Working Paper 2011.02. Brussels: European Trade Union Institute.

Ticktin, M. (2008) 'Sexual violence as the language of border control: Where French feminist and anti-immigrant rhetoric meet', *Signs*, 33, 4, 863-89.

Tin, L.-G. (2015) 'Qui a peur des statistiques ethniques ? Le point de vue de Louis-Georges TIN', *Respect Mag*, 3 May. http://www.respectmag.com/8019-a-peur-statistiques-ethniques

Tyler, I. (2013) *Revolting subjects: Social abjection and resistance in neoliberal Britain.* London: Zed Books.

Unédic (2009) 'Circulaire N° 2009-10 du 22 avril 2009', Paris. http://www.unedic.org/sites/default/files/ci200910.pdf

UNISON (2014) *Counting the cost: How cuts are shrinking women's lives.* London: UNISON.

United Nations Human Rights Commission (2016) 'UN rights experts urge France to protect fundamental freedoms while countering terrorism', Press release, 19 January. www.ohchr.org/EN/NewsEvents/Pages/DisplayNews.aspx?NewsID=16966&LangID=E

Vakil, A.C. (1997) 'Confronting the classification problem: Toward a taxonomy of NGOs', *World Development*, 25, 12, 2057-70.

Veith, B. (2000) 'Les associations locales de femmes étrangères. Multiculturalisme et individuation', *Migrations Société*, 12, 72, 79-88.

Vie Publique (2011) *Non remplacement d'un fonctionnaire sur deux: quel impact?*. http://www.vie-publique.fr/actualite/alaune/non-remplacement-fonctionnaire-deux-quel-impact.html

Wdowiak, L. (2016) 'Nuit Debout: Middle class protests in neoliberal France', LSE Researching Sociology blog. http://blogs.lse.ac.uk/researchingsociology/2016/06/01/middle-class-protests-in-neoliberal-france/

Wearden, G. (2013) 'France and Spain win more time to cut deficits as Europe puts growth over austerity - as it happened', *The Guardian*, 29 May. https://www.theguardian.com/business/2013/may/29/eurozone-crisis-china-imf-ec-deficit

Wekker, G. (2016) *White innocence: Paradoxes of colonialism and race.* Durham: Duke University Press.

Whitely, P., Clarke, H.D., Sanders, D. and Stewart, M.C. (2014) 'The economic and electoral consequences of austerity in Britain', *Parliamentary Affairs*, 68, 1, 4-24.

Wihtol de Wenden, C. and R. Leveau (2001) *La beurgeoisie. Les trois âges de la vie associative issue de l'immigration.* Paris: CNRS Editions.

Winter, B. (2009) *Gender and globalization: Hijab and the Republic: Uncovering the French headscarf debate.* Syracuse, US: Syracuse University Press.

Women's Budget Group (2010) *The impact on women of the Coalition spending review 2010.* http://wbg.org.uk/wp-content/uploads/2016/12/RRB_Reports_4_1653541019.pdf

Women's Budget Group (2012) *The impact on women of the Budget 2012.* wbg.org.uk/wp-content/.../The-Impact-on-Women-of-the-Budget-2012-FINAL.pdf

Zikic, J., Bonache, J. and Cerdin, J.L. (2010) 'Crossing national boundaries: A typology of qualified immigrants' career orientations', *Journal of Organizational Behavior*, 31, 667-86.

Index

Note: Page numbers in *italics* indicate tables and page numbers followed by an n indicate end-of-chapter notes.

contractionary effects 11
co-optation 89–91
Coventry research participants 70, *127*
crises, routinised 39–41
  and austerity measures 41–49
    benefits systems 45–49
    public sector cuts 42–45
cut-throat competition 59, 99

D

decentralisation 105–107
descendent of migrant 50n
devolution 12, 108, 109
difference blindness 2
diversity, approaches to *16*
DIY activism *see* grassroot activism
domestic violence 13, 72, 86, 111–112
droit commun [common law/shared
  right] 71, 102

E

economic crisis *see* 2008 economic
  crisis
Edinburgh research participants
  126–127
  enterprise culture 59, 60–61, 63, 64,
    65
  grassroot activism 80–81, 82
Emejulu, A. 26
employment law *see* labour law, France
empowerment 65–66
England
  2011 English riots 38–39
  activism as self-representation 87
  austerity regime *16*, 17n
  benefits system 47–49
  censorship 102–104
  citizenship model 3
  diversity *16*
  labour market precarity 34–35
  localism agenda 105–106
  minority women activists as
    entrepreneurs 65–70
  public sector cuts 42–43, 44–45
  third sector *16*
    governance 54–58
English riots 2011 38–39
Enlightenment philosophies 20–21
enterprise 53
enterprise culture
  definition 53
  England and Scotland 55

impact on third sector 58, 59–60,
  62–65, 74
minority women activists 65–70
enterprising actors 65
epistemic justice 28–30
epistemic violence of political
  racelessness 23–28
ethnic penalty 34
Europe
  colonialism 19, 21, 22
  political racelessness 19, 115
    Brexit vote 118–120
    burkini ban 117–118
    epistemic justice 28–30
    epistemic violence of 23–28
    migration 121
    racial logic 20–22
    white ignorance and white
      innocence 22–23
European feminism 23–25
European Union 97n
European Women's Lobby 24
exclusionary universalism 26

F

fairness 92
faith-based organisations 113n
family responsibilities 78–79
feminism 23–25, 111–112
femmes relais [intercultural mediators]
  90
fieldwork 123–124
fiscal consolidation policy 46
France
  2005 Paris riots 39
  activism as self-representation 87–89
  austerity regime *16*
  autochthone 50n
  benefits system 45–47
  burkini ban 117–118
  citizenship model 2
  colonialism 88–89, 96–97n
  co-optation 89–93
  descendent of migrant 50n
  diversity *16*
  feminists 23–24
  intersectionality 70–74, 110–111
  labour market precarity 35–36
  loi travail [labour law] 12, 49, 74, 75n
  migrants 50n
  minority group 50n
  poverty 37
  public sector cuts 12, 43
  Socialist Party 12, 72, 89

Printed and bound by CPI Group (UK) Ltd, Croydon, CR0 4YY

09/06/2025

14685898-0004